Praise for
What's Behind Your Brand?

"A must read for any business, brand, or individual who speaks to humans in the year 2024, *What's Behind Your Brand?* is both a 101-guide and a comprehensive deep dive into how to create content that not only sells, but sells in a way that actually works for the world we are living in. As Chief Brand Strategist for a 7-figure company, I will continue to recommend this book to both my team and my clients."

—Michelle Garside
Chief Strategist + Founder, Soul Camp Creative

"Language is everything! Jen is my go-to resource and expert when it comes to the constant evolution of language and what a powerful tool for inclusion it can be. This book lays out all of the opportunities we have to build workplace cultures of belonging through our language—one of the most powerful but underutilized tools we have.

We all need to update our language on an ongoing basis. In this dynamic business environment, I rely on Jen's extensive knowledge and grasp of nuances. Details which can, in these times of great scrutiny for brands, make or break an organization's credibility and reputation."

—Jennifer Brown
DEI Thought Leader, Keynote Speaker,
Bestselling Author of How to Be an Inclusive Leader

"I am thrilled and looking forward to going on another DEIA journey with Dr. Jen O'Ryan. She has a natural ability to call out bias, stereotypes, and gender inequities head on, then break it down for all to understand, followed by providing alternatives to implement a more inclusive and welcoming personal and professional environment."

—Ilona Lohrey
President and CEO,
Greater Seattle Business Association (GSBA)

What's *BEHIND* Your Brand?

A Style Guide for
Humanizing Your Content

Jen O'Ryan, PhD

PYP

Academy
Press

For permission requests, write to the below address:

PYP Academy Press
141 Weston Street, #155
Hartford, CT 06141

The opinions expressed by the Author are not necessarily those held by PYP Academy Press.

Ordering Information: Quantity sales and special discounts are available on quantity purchases by corporations, associations, and others. For details, contact the author at Jen@PagingDrJen.com

Edited by: Caroline Davis & Lori McFerran
Cover design by: Rebecca Pollock
Typeset by: Medlar Publishing Solutions Pvt Ltd., India

Printed in the United States of America.

ISBN: 979-8-218-38626-9 (hardcover)
ISBN: 979-8-218-38613-9 (paperback)
ISBN: 979-8-88797-103-2 (ebook)

Library of Congress Control Number: 2024900470

First edition, February 2024.

Publish Your Purpose is a hybrid publisher of non-fiction books. Our authors are thought leaders, experts in their fields, and visionaries paving the way to social change—from food security to anti-racism. We give underrepresented voices power and a stage to share their stories, speak their truth, and impact their communities. Do you have a book idea you would like us to consider publishing? Please visit PublishYourPurpose.com for more information.

Dedication

This book is dedicated to those who revolutionize spaces that weren't designed with them in mind.

Tiffany —

Enjoy the read !

JROB

Contents

Acknowledgments

Finishing this book was an adventure that involved support, insights, and encouragement from many people. I would like to express my deepest thanks and gratitude to all those who contributed. I could not have brought this across the line without you.

First, I want to thank my family for their support and understanding. These amazing people have shared their grace, perspectives, and humor at the most appropriate times. Paul, countless thanks again. And remember, when I said, "no more books" that Second Editions don't count. Spencer, you are an amazing human, and I couldn't be more proud of you.

Syd, Rachel, and Emily, special thanks for reviewing early versions of this. Your insights and ability to spot sentence fragments continue to amaze me.

I'd also like to thank Jenn T. Grace, founder of Publish Your Purpose. I deeply appreciate your insights and remarkable knack for making this achievable. Both the book and I have greatly benefited from your influence.

Finally, to change agents everywhere, thank you for your interest, curiosity, and efforts. It is my sincere hope that this book proves to be an informative and enjoyable resource.

Introduction

Have you ever watched the show *Bar Rescue* and wondered why people don't do anything about the raw chicken being stored at room temperature? That's what reading through an organization's outdated content can feel like. As though things started out with the best of intentions, only to end up on a digital shelf wondering where it all went wrong.

Style guides provide an established set of rules around structure and mechanics (comma splices, avoiding repetitive word usage, when to semicolon, etc.). They create a framework for how an organization communicates and represents itself to others. Guides can also keep us from having to make decisions. The rules are already there just waiting for our message and ideas to spill out over a template.

A downside to relying on guides is that eventually the world changes. And if no one is tending to the rules, they stagnate. Especially if rules weren't designed to support insights from diverse perspectives. Then, these outdated rules persist as something that just "is."

Attempts to refresh the rules are met with resistance—cost, time, energy, lack of dedicated focus, etc. Small groups of designers will start to go rogue. Adjusting font sizes and sneaking in an Oxford comma occasionally. Increasing the transparency on wildly outdated background colors. Eventually someone in accounting gets wind of a quarterly review that didn't use Times New Roman font and the entire ring gets taken down. But I digress.

I wish I could do a *Bar Rescue*-style reality show, but for mandatory employee training courses. TLC, are you listening?

The truth is, designing effective content is hard. It's also time-consuming and expensive. And now you're adding more things to evaluate and question? Not exactly the type of suggestions that cause executives to rush in, ready to sign checks, and dedicate resources toward.

For some reason, content and materials that companies require people to interact with the most get the least amount of human-focused attention. These materials fall squarely into the "have to" category. Unfortunately, "have to" often translates into "this can be terrible" almost as if terrible is the only option. Myriad reasons and influencing factors play into this. We'll get into those later. Right now, let's focus on the raw chicken in the room.

What tends to get the most attention is content that reflects how an organization or company wants to be perceived. This content includes the macro influencers: self-reflective content like branding, value statements, and unique positioning. Words and images that are carefully crafted, designed, and evaluated to elicit a very intentional response from a specific audience.

But what happens when the messaging works and those potential employees, clients, and customers show up?

Focusing only on the macro causes businesses to miss the micro; those experiential blips on the radar that go largely unnoticed. Micros are all those exchanges and interactions at an individual level. More specifically, the micros with and between individuals who are often largely unnoticed by these same businesses.

Keep in mind, micro doesn't necessarily mean small or less significant. Think of micros as content that reaches more at the individual engagement level as compared to macro, which is that big, seasonal promotion or edgy tagline. If macro is a chainsaw, micro is the scalpel.

When I talk to people about reviewing their micro content, the most common response is "Why?" followed by "Nobody reads those anyway." But people do read them. Often because you require people to read them—or at least "Click to confirm" and acknowledge that they've reviewed the information.

The question shouldn't be "Who reads these anyway?" but rather, "How does the lack of attention to these micro interactions align with an organization's stated values?" Here is a better question: What message is conveyed when micro content isn't only outdated, but offensive or damaging? When negative micro interactions cause potential customers, clients, and employees to go elsewhere.

Why I Decided to Write This

I was driving back from a long day in the desert, trying to stay awake by listening to an audiobook on famous "murder houses" (stop judging). The next chapter started—highlighting a series of unsolved crimes and home invasions. There's something disconcerting besides the seriously messed up story unfolding over my speakers. Whenever the narrator (who is also the author) mentioned the perpetrator, it was with the pronoun "he." As in, "The killer was never caught, and his identity remains a mystery."

Hearing this grammatical tic reminded me of a conversation with a friend about unsolved murders. I am confident that there are more non-male serial killers than conventional wisdom leads us to believe. No matter how contradictory the evidence may be, we are socially conditioned to think of men as the default setting and women as hysterical (yet delicate and adorable) sidekicks.

Therefore, the perpetrator is clearly a man. Sometimes these crimes are committed by a tiny man with size 5 feet. But obviously still a man, nonetheless. While we may never know who committed these heinous crimes, thankfully we can take comfort in knowing that person was absolutely a "he."

Halfway through the introduction, and I'm already off topic. Fantastic.

So, there I was, minding my own business and listening to an audiobook about murder houses. Except I couldn't. Because every time the narrator used "he" when referring to an unknown person or persons, it pulled me out of the story. Either the author of this book has secret insights as to the suspect's identity (which would make the crime solvable), or the writer intentionally decided to use "he" to represent an unknowable aspect of the story.

"GAH! Why isn't there a style guide for writing about gender?!" I shouted into the inky darkness surrounding me. OK, it wasn't that dramatic. I was pulling off the freeway into a suburb of Henderson, Nevada. There were probably streetlights or the comforting blast of neon from a nearby casino. That's not the point.

I realized there isn't a style guide to provide the why and how of designing inclusive content. Not only from a use of pronoun perspective, but how to better represent the experience of being human in our designs and products. A guide on how to create content that is welcoming and available across a broader audience.

From a writing perspective, there is a seemingly endless supply on how to craft a message. There are resources on grammatical rules, improving accessibility, and optimizing for various devices. But very few that provide guidance on how, or more importantly why, to design for inclusion. Or as in the audiobook example, at least ways to avoid being exclusionary.

So I decided to create one. A resource designed to guide you through areas that can detract from your message, or unintentionally create barriers. All while preserving your unique expression, and without overcorrecting into something devoid of creative, impulsive, meaningful art.

All the Different Ways of Being

My second thought as I pulled into the driveway was, "Where is the editor and why didn't they catch this?"

We all have our favorite words. The fallback, go-to words or phrases that creep into our work. Mine is "amazing." Everything is "amazing." If something is good, it's amazing. I can't help it. My copy editor knows this. They gently (sometimes not so gently that it's amazing) remind me that other words exist.

So while this book is geared toward all of you amazing (there it is again) content creators, it's also designed for those who love and support them. People who publish, evaluate, or make purchasing decisions for their employee-facing content. As well as those behind the scenes who edit, proofread, and manage across the entire design process. It involves humans reviewing from different perspectives to spot potential barriers in your product.

People tend to apply criteria or somehow "measure" the inclusiveness and diversity of their content, which can result in predictable, formulaic patterns. This approach can also lead to objectification, stereotyping, and one-dimensional representation. Instead, consider "all the different ways of being."

What do I mean by "all the different ways of being"? Good question. This is the term I use to describe all the different expressions of being human. It's an attempt to encapsulate the complexity of our human experiences because we're never just one thing.

Think of these identities, segments, levels of ability, worldviews, belief systems, lived experiences, and ways of interacting with the world as infinite possible combinations. Each of those possible outcomes is influenced by when and where we were born, how we grew up, what resources or influences we had available to us, which early messages we internalized, and what the world told us each of these elements meant.

Each of us is a culmination of experiences. A unique blend of who we are in the world, influenced by our various roles, and the innate human qualities that make us . . . well, us.

It's a lot, I know. Organizations promote the value of authenticity—showing up as ourselves and creating space for others to do the same. The other side of that authenticity is "seeing" and reflecting people as who they are in the world.

So rather than try to define a list that will invariably leave someone out, I invite you to think about it as all the different ways of being. A multitude of possibilities. Moving through the world in ways you haven't had to consider. Yet.

The approaches to creating inclusive content that I'm describing throughout this book are one part of a much larger toolkit. Figuring out the ideal approach for your content depends on individual goals, available resources, and degree of control over the finished product.

This guide also provides direction on key elements of reviewing and creating content that reaches a broader audience—authentically—while staying consistent with your voice,[1] style, and alignment with your values. I'm not here to

---

[1] "Voice" in this sense describes one's unique communication mode and ways of articulating ideas. This is not intended to limit or erase those who express themselves in ways other than vocally or in spoken language. Different ways of describing this, and similar words with ableist undertones, are noted throughout the book.

change your belief systems. This is about exploring the things that can detract from your message and alternatives to consider along the way.

We'll cover words, images, and phrases that are (however unintentionally)

- offensive

- grounded in, or perpetuating, stereotypes

- damaging or harmful

- misrepresenting or appropriating cultures and/or other ways of being (typically marginalized or historically excluded populations)

I'm also going to invite you to notice the absences. Who isn't being represented or considered in the design and final product? Bias is often demonstrated by what is not there. Ever try to prove a negative? Right, it's like that. When the absence of something is expected or common, it's perceived to be "normal."

Conventional Wisdom of Style

I started working on this book by returning to the basics: reading various guides on writing. Going through the books that permeate our libraries and school systems, the ones that make up the fundamentals of common stylistic reference materials. Eventually, my review made its way to *Elements of Style* by Strunk and White (EOS, 2023).

Revisiting *Elements of Style* felt like having lunch with an old relative or driving around the neighborhood where I grew up.

Familiar, yet smaller and less imposing than I remembered. The areas I'd long since forgotten about were still there (both of us now older and less relevant). Even in the later editions, undertones of sexism, classicism, and stereotypes are evident. It was condescending at best, and blatantly dismissive of everyone who was not on Team *Elements*.

As I got further into the history and various editions, I started to lose focus. More and more of my attention was going toward how bad the guidance was. I realized that, rather than reviewing the information, I was building a case against it. Deconstructing each example of erasure and contempt for people who weren't like them.

My take down was getting so good. I had a point-by-point dissection of outdated ideas, shining a light on how damaging these rules were. All the reasons for needing to move away from using this as standard, but to what end?

I had fallen into a familiar trap—building a case to expose the "wrongness" of an existing framework. Charging up that metaphorical hill and shouting at the gate about the power of language, and then demonstrating the gaps and biased representation built into these rules.

But, why? With most change resisters, it's unlikely that arguments alone will result in a different perspective. So, who benefits from that approach?

Directing energy toward deconstruction can be necessary. It can be enjoyable in a "cake for breakfast" kind of way. However, it can also lure your focus away from innovation and solving the underlying problem; distracting you from creating a new, viable alternative that sparks the next disruption.

Where I would be better off directing my energy was in writing a new style guide to fill the gap. Develop a resource that people can reference when they want their content and message to be welcoming across a broader audience; both for those who understand that there are barriers, and those who haven't needed to think about it.

Instead of continuing this deconstructive approach, I took my own advice. "Trying to convince somebody that everything they believe is 'wrong' is not effective." (And, yes, I am putting this on a coffee cup. Keep reading to learn about how to preorder.)

I'm not writing this to convince Team Strunk and White of anything. I'm creating this to provide you (and hopefully others) with a set of resources for creating content through the lens of Inclusion, Diversity, and Representation. This is a starting point and ongoing guide to reference as you develop messaging that **brings people in**.

The intention behind this book is to show you where barriers like to hide and the different ways that bias can show up; to provide practical application and examples that illustrate how to make the shift. And how to do all of this while bringing others along the way.

You might be thinking to yourself, "This is all great information, but why am I reading it? What does any of this have to do with grammar, punctuation, and a style guide?"

Excellent questions.

As you work through this book, you're going to start noticing things in content. Absences, outdated terms, cringy expressions—all of it. You might apply a different lens when evaluating style rules and conventional wisdom. As your perception begins to change, this book offers alternatives to consider throughout the design cycle.

We don't have to settle for century-old writing styles steeped in traditions that were never intended to support everyone to begin with. They didn't represent everyone then, and certainly don't today.

Don't work on this type of employee- or customer-facing content? Stick around anyway. The pointers, things to avoid, and guidance apply to a variety of product types. While the final outcome is different, you might find elements that relate from design through post-launch support.

Let's revisit the murder house audiobook example.

Another plausible, yet annoying, reason for the author's choice of using "he" is related to stylized writing norms, dating back to the early 1900s. Possibly as far back as the dawn of time, but this is difficult to substantiate.

Traditional writing guidelines dictated who was seen, how they were portrayed, and which expressions were "proper" or "professional." They kept the system of "acceptable" writers (and messages) in place.

Guides, such as *Elements of Style*, established rules for writing, covering everything from avoiding split infinitives to specific word usage. According to this conventional wisdom, using "he" as the default pronoun is more correct.

While the guidance has adjusted slightly since the 1970s edition, "he" as the standard for representation persists even in *Elements of Style: Classic Edition* (Strunk & De A'Morelli, 2018).

> A common inaccuracy is the use of the plural pronoun when the antecedent is a distributive expression such as each, each one, everybody, everyone, many a man, which, though implying more than one person, requires the pronoun to be in the singular.
>
> Similar to this, but with even less justification, is the use of the plural pronoun with the antecedent anybody, anyone, somebody, someone, the intention being either to avoid the awkward "he or she," or to avoid committing oneself to either.
>
> Some bashful speakers even say, "A friend of mine told me that they, etc." Use he with all above words, unless the antecedent is or must be feminine. (Strunk & De A'Morelli, 2018, p. 81–82)

Think this writing standard is some old-timey throwback to the 1950s? Try 2018.

Gender is far from the only aspect of identity erased and stereotyped in representation, but it is one of the features I'm using as an example throughout the book. Both because it is often the least meaningful way to segment humans and because language around gender is so influential. It shapes how we interact with each other and how we interpret ourselves in the world.

Hold on to that thought for a minute. We're going to get there.

Before We Get Started

The first rule of Inclusion Club: you have to intentionally stay open to different perspectives and ways of being. If you want people to show up authentically as who they are, then be open to "seeing"[2] them for who they are and interacting with them as they are. Otherwise, it just doesn't work.

The second rule of Inclusion Club is that you have to intentionally stay open to different perspectives and ways of being. (See what I did there? Now that quote from *Fight Club* will be stuck in your head. If you have it available to you, please experience the rest of this book in Brad Pitt's voice. I couldn't afford him for the narration.)

This openness also applies to those who don't agree with you on inclusion, diversity, and representation as well as those who don't understand the need for anything to change at all. Diverse perspectives by default include people who don't agree with you.

Keep this in mind when navigating different sections of the book. Because the following chapters contain elements, thoughts, suggestions, and musings that might cause real or metaphorical eye rolling or vocalized responses of "gaahhhh-hhzzzzzz, you can't be serious" (or similar).

---

[2] Throughout this book, words like "seeing" and "seen" will sometimes appear in quotation marks. Primarily because "see" in this context implies using our visual capacity and related sensory perception. However, not everyone has the same physical ability. Using the word "see" presupposes unimpaired vision. It excludes the experience of those who interact with the world differently. It also normalizes using "see" when more precise (and inclusive) words are available.

Have that experience. Sit with any discomfort. Work through a crossword puzzle together. Feel all the feels. Same for any "Why are people so sensitive?" thoughts. Then, give that eye roll a hug and send it on its way, because we have work to do. You picked up this book for a reason.

It takes time to sit with a reaction and evaluate what's coming up. I invite you to lean into this process and peel back the experience. What might cause that strong response? Where did it come from? Now incorporate all those new insights and use them to process future reactions.

And remember, I'm not here to change your mind or undo belief systems. This is a partnership. Like the colleague who gestures nonchalantly at lunch to caution about that bit of salad stuck between your teeth. This is an invitation to consider how to connect and incorporate different ways of being human into your work.

As unlikely as it may seem, you can make small changes that shift an entire organization. Then positive shifts become contagious, making larger change possible as people feel more positive, engaged, and "seen."

How to Use This Book

So far, we've covered a bit about what this book is. I'd also like to talk briefly about what it *isn't*.

This book is not about erasure. Or blanding everything down to a generic, joyless snooze-fest. It's not about becoming "woke," or cancel culture, or political correctness run amok.

This is not another session on all the things you're doing wrong or the things you have to do according to your Human Resources department.

This is not a brand guide, where font size, color, and ratios are tightly defined. There isn't a list of checkboxes. It isn't introducing yet another set of "rules." Except in extreme examples, this book doesn't provide a prescriptive set of "always/never" guidelines. It's not the end and final resource. Our understanding is constantly evolving. By the time this edition is published, at least one thing will have changed or been expanded.

This book is not a lot of things. Because rigidity is not how humans operate. More importantly, it isn't how representation—*authentic* representation—works.

More than anything, this book is intended to be a resource. A viable alternative to those who find a gap between "traditional" style guides and designing content that brings people in. Conveying a message where your clients, employees, and customers are genuinely reflected.

What I've found in doing this work is that most organizations don't notice there's a problem. Rarely does bad content spring from malicious intent. Can it? Absolutely. But we're focused on the middle of that bell curve: people who think their content is welcoming, or at least okay enough to get by. Maybe they don't prioritize the micros in favor of macros. Or they simply don't know where to look for bad content.

It's not like executives are lining up to learn why their annual employee training is offensive, or enthusiastically reading through all the new hire documents. It's boring, tedious, and worst of all expensive to dedicate the time needed. A lack of resources, expertise, and commitment from leadership are only a few obstacles that keep organizations from doing the work. Sprinkle in economic uncertainties, employee burn-out, and the complex relationship people have with change to begin with—it's a wonder anything happens at all.

Lastly, this book is designed with a "chose your own adventure" approach.

Ever try to find a recipe online? Or something basic like the right temperature to cook salmon? A post pops up with an intriguing title. You click it, then spend 17 minutes scrolling through an origin story. The author has so much personally invested in sharing details, they forget that some readers are looking for the payout. We are looking for the end point information and don't always have time for a journey. This book has elements beyond just a recipe but is organized in a way that promotes skipping around.

Yes, there is a lot of discussion and supporting information. I've included sections on overcoming resistance and bringing others along on the journey. There is a lot of information on the "why" behind the "how" of designing more inclusive content. Navigating change, where to focus your energy, and how to introduce new approaches are in here as well.

So if you want to head directly to the recipe, that's OK too. I get it. We're all trying to keep the business moving forward. This information is here when you need it. The chapters are organized to be stand-alone resources. This isn't a linear process. And salmon should be baked at 350°F—unless you prefer it a little crispy. Then 400°F. Or consider grilling.

Chapter One

Things to Consider, Part One

I used to do hot yoga. It was one of my favorite ways to completely unplug. After several years of practicing, I was getting pretty good at holding poses without falling over. So proud. During a particularly incident-free session, the instructor came over to me during a pose.

"Can I adjust you?" he asked. Consent is important. I nodded, as yoga is quiet time, and he pressed gently on my lower back. I moved less than an inch, but suddenly everything fell into place.

From my internal vantage point, I was doing the pose exactly as instructed. However, to an objective observer, with decades of experience and a trained eye, something in my posture was an eighth of an inch off. Which was preventing me from getting the full benefit of this pose.

Slight adjustment and the entire experience changed.

Had that instructor used a different approach, or if I wasn't in a mindset to receive the adjustment, this exchange would have another ending. So, as with most meaningful changes, it all starts with you.

Why a New Approach? And Why Now?

Let's start this off with a little introspection. Ask yourself: What is motivating you to pick up a style guide on inclusion, diversity, and representation? And how does that align with why your company or organization decided to prioritize this?

Take a few minutes to reflect on it. Why focus on this specific area at this point in time?

Don't overthink it. There is no wrong or right answer. Reflecting on the "whys" gives you a starting point. Outlining your thoughts will establish a baseline intention. One which is likely to change as you get deeper into the process.

Is the goal to position yourself as a better business partner in the community? Is there a nagging sense that your content could be better, but improving it is too overwhelming on top of everything else? Perhaps you're looking for a way to influence change. Maybe you were simply handed a directive by the leadership team, and now you have to execute (in which case, keep the receipt, you should totally expense this book). All of these are valid reasons.

As you go through the content here, check in occasionally on those initial thoughts. Especially when things aren't going to plan. It helps to reflect on what's pushing you forward, as well as what might be holding you back. These early motivations can also help mitigate burnout by keeping the bigger objective in perspective. You're setting (and resetting) an intention throughout the process.

I also ask these "why now" questions because their responses will often inform how people navigate the book. This is going to be a bumpy ride and not everyone is going to agree with the changes you are trying to make. Inclusion, diversity, and representation can spark some very emotionally charged conversations. It can tap into belief systems that people might not realize they have.

What Are You Trying to Convey?

Designing inclusive, diverse, and representative content starts with asking yourself two very different questions: What are you trying to convey? How might I experience this as . . . ?

Part of exploring these two questions is to build a habit of intentionality. If our primary motivation is getting a message out quickly, with minimal friction, we will consistently fall back to a shortlist of default terms and generic images. This approach is great in an emergency. Establishing trust and engaging across a broad audience? Not so much.

The problem is that we are always in a hurry to get a message out.

Flying through our coffee order, waiting for the dot-dot-dot of our friend texting so we can respond, relying on familiar buzzwords when sending out a company-wide email about whatever new policy change is coming—our brains interpret all these messages as too urgent for vocabulary reflection time.

We've become conditioned to process this way in our interruption-based culture of "busy."

Complicating things further, our brains are optimized to conserve energy. People tend to stick with the same words, using them over and over, without really thinking about it. Locating the precise word or phrase to convey your message takes time and focus.

So now we have one person flinging grab-n-go words that worked for them since the eighth grade, and an equally distracted recipient trying to extract meaning from those words while multitasking on their phone. Side note, we're not good at multitasking. At least not when it comes to more complex functions like deriving nuance from language.

Where was I going with that? Right: precision and intentional language.

Exploring this aspect isn't about getting to a "right" answer. It's about emphasizing the influence of words and images as potential barriers to your message. To creatively explore if there is a more precise word choice that brings people in, rather than excluding them, and elicits the action or response you intended.

The task here is to evaluate your word choice. It isn't an always/never situation. ATM has a broad, shared understanding and is infinitely easier to convey than "automated teller machine." However, if your message is lacking enough social familiarity, or the context provided by surrounding words is not clear, it puts people at a disadvantage.

Keep in mind, what you intended can be vastly different from what is received. Our habits of taking mental shortcuts also apply to how we receive and process information. We are constantly filtering and applying value judgments without realizing it. And while we might have a common definition available for individual words, humans do not always have a shared understanding and application of them.

How Might I Experience This As . . . ?

The second question to consider is "How might I experience this as . . . ?" The "as . . ." represents everyone who is not you. People who move through the world and experience it differently than you, or those in your circle of influence.

Most creators and product owners are familiar with this exercise—trying to identify and describe the needs of their ideal buyer or target audience. It typically involves a series of statements like this:

"As an ideal buyer, I want to do . . ." or "As an ideal buyer, I need to understand . . ."

The problem in this is an underlying assumption that these individuals experience a similar world as the designer. Creators and product owners forget to consider, "As a potential buyer, how might I experience this?" That path of exploration is the very heart of this guide.

Think about the last thing you designed, created, or developed.

Did your process include exploring any of the following?

- As a queer person, how might I experience an event web page with images portraying only straight couples?

- As a person of color, how might I experience your "commitment to diversity" statement being presented by an all-white board of directors who are of similar age and background?

- As a dyslexic person, how might I experience the huge blocks of text on your help page?

- As someone who is not a man, how might I experience a CEO who always starts meetings with "Hey guys"?

- As a trauma survivor with PTSD, how might I experience the videos in your company's mandatory anti-harassment course?

The purpose of "how might I experience this as . . ." is to disrupt internalized default settings that are influencing your design.

Please don't attempt to answer this question directly. The question itself represents being mindful of lived experience outside of your own. Reflecting on this opens the door to recognizing there are different ways of being. It reminds you to be intentional throughout the process and to consider that your message, content, etc. will be consumed through other perspectives.

Exploring this question does not mean categorizing people based on one or two features. Or generalizing an interpretation of the entire population. Or presuming to know the lived experience of another person. Everyone's lens is uniquely their own. This is also a good place to think about the types of expertise needed when bridging these gaps in your understanding.

One example of, "How might I experience this as . . ." are curb cuts, the gradual ramp features at most sidewalk corners. Initially promoted by Jack Fisher (ILI, 1999) these seemingly minor structural changes have significant impact for a wide variety of humans. People with mobility or balance differences, pushing heavy carts or strollers, and a variety of other situations.

Curb cuts are now synonymous with a concept known as "Universal Design" (UD, 2023). Principles of Universal Design promote removing barriers and increasing product accessibility.

Let's go back to noticing the absences for a minute. Most pedestrians don't consciously think about the difficulties and barriers created by curb design. Those who, for whatever reason, haven't witnessed or experienced anything but simply stepping up or down. They've never had to consider this as a physical barrier, or the short- and long-term impacts of curb impediments on others.

People in this category might initially be resistant to changes like curb cuts. The perception of curb cuts having limited benefit or being unnecessary—especially given the cost, time, and inconvenience during construction—need to be overcome before change is possible. Even when these changes result in demonstrably improved outcomes for those who directly benefit, as well as those who can continue not having to think about navigating curbs.

This example is not to create an either/or trade-off or false equivalency between abilities and access. It's to illustrate the importance of bringing people along on this journey. Shaping perspective helps others understand the "why" behind change. Hopefully this book will provide resources you can tap to overcome the various flavors of resistance.

A key outcome when you invoke these two questions during the design process is the removal of barriers that limit access or exclude.

Except you're going to take things a bit further. Your content is going to actively **bring people in**.

Now, let's tie this idea back to an actual design decision.

Imagine you're tasked with designing an application to improve the experience for new gym members. After all the extensive research, proof of concept, development, testing, market research, go-to-market plans, reviews with legal, etc., this massive undertaking was finally ready for the world.

Everything was executed beautifully. It was well received. Right up until it wasn't.

As part of the registration process, users were prompted to enter their gender. The options they had to select from were "male," "female," or "other." This detail—tiny seconds of interaction—was asking people to designate themselves as other.

In the larger discussion and post-launch evaluation of success, this registration feature was measured by one criterion:

"Did it function?" If "yes" was higher than the acceptable threshold, it was a hit.

Until I extracted that display experience as an image. "Here's a snapshot of what your customer encounters. They are required to choose from 'male, female, or other.' If not, they abandon registration. Does anyone have data on abandon rates at this stage of the process?"

Now seems like a good time to mention the number of awkward questions involved in this work, which is slightly more than the number of awkward pauses you'll learn to sit with while people process.

All that effort, the resources invested, financial risk . . . everything comes down to what a member experiences as they interact across the entire process. This one question tells them everything they need to know about your organization. The user chooses the least distasteful option or decides to abandon registration altogether and move on with life.

Unless you know where and how to measure, this abandonment insight will disappear along with that former customer. Abandonment rates that could have alerted someone to test the registration process and find this problematic decision. Inclusion or exclusion lives in all those tiny points along the life cycle.

Before we transition away from this section, I'd like to leave you with another example. Picture three friends hanging out in a distant city. Looking for adventure and . . . wait, that might be a song. Hang on.

So, there we were, having just scored last-minute tickets to an intriguing show. As we approached the box office, the attendant, who was charged with stamping for admission, was cheerfully shouting, "Wrists, hands, or foreheads!" It was somehow a question and instructions at the same time. And it made my heart very happy. Because that person was considering other ways of being.

Not everyone has hands. Or wrists. Or skin that they want to expose for any number of reasons.

This example shows how you can be inclusive without overengineering or singling out any one individual. It's about being intentional with your choice of words. About staying mindful to all the different ways of being. And then considering how individuals might experience interactions with your product, service, or experience.

What is the intended outcome of stamping someone in this example? You need to apply a visible mark that indicates they've paid admission. That's it. That's the objective.

So, rather than overcorrect (single out) by listing all the reasons that someone might not have hands, or possibly doesn't want to take their gloves off in the freezing cold, you state options for stamping. You use words in a way that brings people in.

People have control over their choice, rather than having to explain a situation. Inclusion means opening up alternatives without putting the burden on an individual.

Did the attendant intend this message to signal inclusion? That doesn't matter (although, yes, they did). The important point is that this message makes the experience welcoming and available to a broader audience. Without needlessly drawing unwanted attention on someone or overcomplicating things.

For the majority of people who get their hands stamped without thinking about it, they will continue not having to think about it.

For those who dread this specific interaction, it might be a refreshing surprise. The realization that they don't have to try and navigate, explain, endure, subject themselves to the awkward or unkind words from others just to enter a venue.

It takes a minute to realize that you've unintentionally been excluding or making someone self-conscious. Take that opportunity to flip the script.

Best part of this example? The "splash and ripple" effect. Every person who noticed that shift in language takes the message with them. Like I have here. And now like you can after reading this.

The Message Is Rarely Just a Message

Pop quiz. What is this?

Yes, it's an icon. But what does it represent? "Save." Outstanding.

So, this depiction of a floppy disc represents the action "to save." Next question: Who's used a floppy disc in the last 5 or 6 years? Or 10? Or ever?

People typically know that the object pictured on "save" button icons is a floppy disc; it's an antiquated symbol for the action represented. This image stopped meaning floppy disc and started meaning "save" a very long time ago. Yet it persists, because we agree that it adequately represents a meaning. Or it's at least close enough to prevent bothering about it.

We have a shared understanding of meaning even though many of the users engaging with this icon are several generations removed from the object's use. An action represented by something that is no longer relevant to our understanding, or how we interact with the world now.

Much in the same way you can get generational differences when asking if it's a "pound sign" or a "hashtag." The answer is yes.

So, I want you to start thinking about all symbols and imagery that you use to communicate meaning. Then consider what other messages are coming along with them.

For example, when you see this symbol and think how archaic it is:

Apply it to this symbol as well, because it's the same thing.

We've absorbed these images and collectively recognize them to mean men or women. It's a visual representation that we've constructed meaning around, and it helps us navigate the world more quickly.

Except is that really everything this image represents? Let's pull the lens back for a minute. Remember, this is about considering experiences or worldviews outside of your own.

Here are a few elements involved with the example image above:

- It presents gender as a binary. There are men and women. That's it.

- Women are differentiated with a dress-like triangle over their torso.

If we were to interpret this symbol directly, it indicates one designated area or facility for those wearing a dress, tunic, or giant triangle and a second area for those who are not.

Describing women and men as the only two possible options creates an either/or condition for your audience. If this is causing a response for you, now might be a good time to revisit that earlier section on the "Why a new approach, and why now?"

It isn't that there aren't men and women. There are men and women. It's that there aren't **only** men and women. Images that create an either/or are excluding your clients or employees who are nonbinary, agender, gender fluid, or just really don't like the stereotypes of only humans who wear dresses can go into this area.

Imagine creating a similar image to represent short versus tall. We can understand these two words to be relational. Taller or shorter than something else? Sure, however, creating an icon to indicate tall means having a shared understanding of what represents that.

Which brings us back to the two exploratory questions—what you are trying to convey and how might it be experienced. Evaluate where, given the context, the default image creates a barrier or excludes. Does your audience see themselves reflected in the message? How are they being represented there?

Hold that thought for now—we'll come back to it.

Chapter Two

Things to Consider, Part Two

Words mean things. It's good to get that one out of the way. While we might have a common definition available for individual words formed through a series of characters, our interpretations of their intended meanings are influenced by other factors.

Body language, tone, and social or cultural subtext all have an impact on derived meaning. If you've traveled to Texas and had someone say, "Well, bless your heart," you know what I'm talking about.

Our brains make meaning from context by combining surrounding words and images. Supporting words and imagery enhance our understanding of the key message. You may have observed this when struggling through a new language or watching someone learn to read. If you encounter an unfamiliar word, the first impulse is to search for context from what else is available.

Ladies and Dandies

Our understanding of conventional writing styles and business language has evolved in some ways, but not all.

Let's go back to social subtext for a minute. While waiting to catch a flight at the airport recently, I was having an animated conversation with my travel companion about inclusive greetings. True story: My personal and professional goal is to convince Delta Airlines to stop saying "ladies and gentlemen" at the beginning of every announcement. Exciting, I know.

The problem with "ladies and gentlemen," other than the exclusion of those who are neither ladies nor gentlemen, is the social implications associated with "ladies."

While "ladies" might not seem like a loaded term, it comes with an underlying set of social expectations: acceptable behaviors, degree of agency, mannerisms, speaking style, amount of space one can take up.

You might be asking yourself, but what about "gentlemen"? Doesn't that term also have social expectations and baggage? Sure, right up until you are deciding between visiting a "ladies' club" or a "gentlemen's club." Do these hypothetical clubs create similar mental images?

Yeah, my colleague didn't agree with my example either. So I took a different approach.

If "ladies and gentlemen" is acceptable and without social subtext, what if the greeting was "ladies and dandies"?

For those unfamiliar with the term, Merriam-Webster defines dandy as "of, relating to, or suggestive of a man who gives exaggerated attention to personal appearance" (MW, n.d.). Encyclopedia.com includes this in its definition of "dandy," a name for a man who pays great attention to dress and fashion and often dresses with a flamboyant style" (ENC, n.d.).

That lands a little differently, doesn't it?

The point was easier for my colleague to relate to when he was represented by an image that was completely foreign to his identity, his sense of self. It doesn't have to be dandies. Pick any other generalized representation that limits, inaccurately depicts, or doesn't reflect the population. More specifically, it doesn't convey your intended message. This is default setting, go-to wording.

Words mean things, and these meanings are enhanced by social context. Creating a bias that we accept as inherently normal.

For those who are consistently reflected in ways that align with their identity, it can be easy to forget how intrinsically one's sense of self is connected to how people are represented at the macro (societal) level; until they find themselves represented by an image that's discordant with their identity.

The words we use and encounter shape how we think and perceive. They tell us the social space we are expected to occupy, who is represented and in what way, and how to interact with others. Words and expressions that inhabit our lives influence how we interpret ourselves (and others) in the world.

The influence of social context is easier to relate to when applied to words and phrases from a few generations ago. Flip through any book on writing standards from the 1970s. Starting a message with "Dear Sir or Madam" was the pinnacle of English business communication. Anything less was considered unprofessional.

If it feels awkward to start an email with "Dear Sir or Madam," imagine a similar response when using "ladies and gentlemen."

This is where we tap into that incredible capacity and power of language. You're aiming for intentional word choice. What, specifically, are you trying to convey? How might this be experienced by someone who is not you?

Delta, if you're listening, might I suggest the following alternatives: "Hello, Delta passengers." "Good morning and welcome!" "Hey, Peeps!" Or just start talking. We know who we are.

Conjure—How Our Brains Shape Meaning

We discussed earlier how our brains look for additional context to help us interpret. This process is a big part of how humans make meaning, and it becomes increasingly more complex when combining words with images.

Huge oversimplification alert

The following is a high-level description of an exceptionally complex process. Human brains are tricky systems and each one manages information differently. Interpreting meaning does not necessarily happen in a linear process. All of us store and retrieve information differently. This generalized overview helps depict how we prioritize and navigate messages.

Our brains make meaning by combining all the information available. We tend to start by processing the "easy" parts first. Environmental cues, like where I am (work, school, train station?) and what my goal is in the given situation (scanning a sign showing the building's emergency route during a fire vs. reviewing it for regulatory compliance).

Then we start to interpret the message by applying our understanding to the images and any words provided. Words are more complex than images; those are either pulled in last or maybe sprinkled in as we process the image.

Yes, I understand that letters are symbols. For the purposes of this exercise, think of symbols in terms of representing a concept (a "stop" indicator, currency, the "save" buttons, warning of poison or danger, etc.), and separate them from letters.

Humans take in the primary image or symbol, and then look for patterns. Position of the image, font style and color, and social or cultural subtext will also influence our interpretation. At this point, we've already attached some level of meaning based on the image and environment. Meaning takes shape before we get to words. In some cases, we go with this level of meaning and skip words entirely. Remember, words are complex, and brains are optimized for efficiency.

How many times have you scrolled down a web page looking for the "help" or "download" button without reading anything else? Or tossed out the instruction guide for assembling that bookshelf only to retrieve it later once you've been reduced to sputtering angrily at a hex key (or Allen wrench, depending on your imprint).

That's our brains latching onto available images and seeking out the path of least resistance. We glean information from looking at the steps and try to assemble bookshelves without investing energy in reading words that provide details. It's based on images plus our desired outcome and drive to complete a task. Why waste time and energy processing words? We're in a hurry to get messages in, the same way we are to get them out.

If we absolutely must process words, that stage comes next. The supporting words enhance our understanding of the key message—or at least the supporting words that we read. Remember, we're still looking for ways to conserve energy. So, the positioning and emphasis of supporting words also factors in our meaning.

We build meaning by attributing value and making associations based on our previous experiences, internal biases, social conditioning, and how we interpret ourselves or others in the world.

That's our implicit bias—how the brain filters and applies value judgments without our realizing it—being partnered up with our desire to cut corners and get to an end as quickly as possible. Like the plot of every terrible Odd Couple movie from the 1980s.

The best word I've found to describe this experience is "conjure." Your brain is summoning a meaning. One that serves the purpose of making sense of the message, while also reinforcing our existing beliefs and understanding of the world.

The scary aspect of this is how much of the attachment, association, and enhancement operates outside of our awareness.

The brain helps us interpret the world by summoning previous mental imprints, memories, and anything else we have stored away. I'm separating mental imprints from memories here because humans don't always consciously or accurately remember every experience and early message. The brain doesn't retrieve these pieces of information in the same way that we think of memories.

This might be a good time to revisit the huge oversimplification disclaimer from a few pages back. I'm sharing a generalized view of human processing to illustrate the degree to which design is unconsciously influenced by each individual's worldview and belief systems. And how seemingly innocuous images or word choice can detract from your intended message. Content doesn't have to reach a level of blatantly offensive to be harmful or damaging.

Where was I? Ah, yes, conjuring.

We make connections between our internal information set and the message being presented to us. This creates an opportunity for creative license. Our brain "conjures" meaning that isn't immediately or explicitly present in the content. At least not to those without specific pieces of information that are available to us through lived experience and previous interpretations.

Conjure = internal processing + positioning (images + text)

This happens through:

- combinations of words and images

- attribution (applying characteristics, traits, value judgments, and motivations without evidence present to support)

- the relative position, proportion, and placement of word/images

- emphasis of words or placement near other images

- association and categorization by grouping

- everything else that leads up to, and follows, the message

Combining words, images, and positioning to conjure negative associations can be intentional. Content designed to convey a negative message, but presented in a way that creates an element of plausible deniability or an exit strategy. Negative messages can also be unintentional which is still problematic, but somewhat easier to fix and avoid in the future. The same is true of word choice and using specific terms to imply a meaning indirectly.

In content, you are conveying a message through words, images, patterns, and symbols. The recipient is conjuring meaning through an array of subtle details, filtered through their imprint.

Conjuring taps into our unconscious processing system to make meaning. We do this when the words and images support what our bias expects, and when the pattern or expectation is disrupted. Humans tend to skim over expected patterns and only notice things that contradict or don't align. For example, stereotypes and bias that fit a reader's experience will go unnoticed (except to reinforce the confirmation).

In order to disrupt the bias, we need to interrupt the patterns.

A disrupted bias works like this: if the reader expects to encounter "he" and a depiction of an older white male when the word "pilot" is used, any other representation elicits a flash response of "What the hell?" The further away an outcome is from what our bias anticipated, the stronger this "What the hell?" response is. Same when the outcome conflicts with our deeply internalized bias of how things are "supposed to be."

Disruption creates a kind of tension in the user. It's a surprise that pulls the brain back from autopilot. Something changed, or an unexpected association appeared and flagged the user to assess this new information. An unexpected behavior or trait in what had been a consistent and reliable pattern.

Absent any other information, people tend to project themselves onto characters when reading or listening to a story. Humans apply mental images to stories that are a close reproduction of the world they move through.

Have you ever created an image of characters when reading a book, then the movie comes out and it completely upends what you've conjured? Right, it's like that.

Your role in this as the designer is to unwind bias, even as it causes people—including you—to experience these disruptions. On the other side of that disruption is more meaningful representation of humans. Your message will reflect and welcome a larger audience.

These conjured meanings tap into our internal bias with so much subtlety that it goes largely unnoticed at a conscious level. The underlying meaning is still picked up by our internal processing and slowly reinforces that existing bias.

Keep in mind, these existing biases are reinforced for everyone who encounters them. Meaning that negative associations, however unintentional, remind everyone who they are in the world and how to interact with each other.

Conjured representations perpetuate stereotypes, reinforce gender and racial biases, and convey an impression about the message's source—in this case, your organization.

That message is going to tell them everything they need to know about . . .

- you
- your Company
- what it's like to work with you
- what it's like to do business with you

The good news about conjuring is that it also works with positive association. Making a positive association requires a very intentional focus and appreciation of how everything fits together. This gets us deeper into the nuance of removing barriers in your message. How to make meaning and disrupt conjuring by reviewing for the "whole."

But first, you'll have to work through a few things. Part of working with content is to increase the likelihood of spotting things that others don't. Navigating yourself through this internal process is one thing. Leading a team of product owners and decision-makers on this journey takes more effort. If completing your work depends on other people or teams, it's easy to lose track of why things keep derailing.

So, treat problematic content as the design flaw that it is.

It's a Design Flaw, Not a "Blind Spot"

The expression "blind spot" is often used to describe how bias blocks or influences our perspective. I think this misses the point. It also frames our bias as somehow being separate from us.

An obstruction or limitation indicates that you *can't* see it. Bias means that you *don't* see it. There is a capacity for awareness, but not the exposure (through a lifetime of personal lived experience, early messages, and multigenerational influences) to notice it. We're about to change all that.

Design flaws are those pesky things that might technically work, but don't support what the person needs to accomplish. These flaws range anywhere from annoying to fatal.

John Spacey describes these as, "A design that fails to meet requirements or serve customer needs . . . In many cases, they introduce unnecessary risk, damage brand reputation, or result in poor product ratings and sales" (Spacey, 2017).

Problematic content, exclusionary word choice, bias, and erasure all fit into this description. Unless the intended user experience was to exclude, cause harm, or perpetuate stereotypes. In which case, you probably need a different book instead of this one.

Thinking about these examples as design flaws does a couple of things. First, it diffuses some of the emotionally charged resistance. Design flaws are objective and have a business justification behind correcting them. Remember, not everyone is coming from the same point of the journey. Do I wish we could just point out systemic racism in materials and have it fixed? Yes. But if it were that easy, we wouldn't still be having this conversation.

Second, considering problematic content or design as flaws makes it part of the quality control process. It's a quality issue with potential harm to users and likely to have a negative impact on reviews, market expansion, and brand reputation.

This approach also creates new opportunities for review points, cross-checks, and a system that can adapt to future needs. As our understanding evolves, so do the mechanisms that support our products.

It starts by understanding resistance and how to bring others along.

People Are More Rationalizing Than Rational

Humans can cling to dysfunction like Kate Winslet on that giant door in the movie *Titanic*.

People have an incredible ability to resist change, even when operating in toxic or dysfunctional environments. They may be uncomfortable with the situation, but they understand it. They know how to exist and interact within the system, even when it's detrimental to one's well-being.

People will rationalize clinging to ideas and systems that are objectively broken, if these ideas and systems:

- fill a void or meet a need

- provide them a false sense of control

- protect them from overwhelm or emotional distress

- prevent them from confronting unprocessed experiences or trauma

Depending on how deeply their sense of self is intertwined with the situation, individuals can encourage others to rationalize it as well. They can derail conversations and point to any variety of scenarios that could be worse. As people begin to accept the experience as "normal," it becomes increasingly more difficult to imagine how things could be different.

Are you starting to wonder what this has to do with a style guide on content? People can have very big feelings about grammar changes. Take a few minutes to do an internet search on the "Oxford comma debate." Go ahead, I'll wait.

Right?! Big feelings!

Full disclosure, I am firmly on #TeamOxfordComma. Even before it became the determining factor in a 2017 litigation that resulted in an award of $5 million to plaintiffs in a dispute involving unpaid overtime (BBC, 2022).

Now imagine the level of controversy sparked by suggesting the default pronoun should be something other than "he." Exactly. Language shapes how we interpret the world. The degree to which people gravitate toward or away from challenging structures varies greatly.

And don't kid yourself into thinking this is a generational thing. We're only one generation away from when left-handed kids were forced to write with their nondominant hands. Because obviously writing with your left hand leads to demonic possession (MW, 2016).

Language evolves, as does our approach to constructing a message. Advertisements from previous decades are perfect examples of what used to be considered "acceptable." If not acceptable, at least condoned. Or the opposition was silenced by those with more power.

Most of us have dealt with these situations. We keep ourselves stuck because doing something else is too scary, unknown, or seemingly impossible. It's part of being human. This isn't an invitation to diagnose your colleagues. The one approach less effective than telling someone, "Everything you believe is wrong," is slapping a label on their behavior.

Label-slapping also lets you skip directly to a solution without doing the groundwork. I'm including it here as a potential influence when you are faced with the question, "Why does change feel so impossible sometimes?"

So, what happens when your content is trapped by resistance to change or toxic rationalization? Well, you could trot out some ads from the 1950s or host a screening of the movie *9 to 5* to provide points of comparison.

Alternatively, you can build a kit of resources to substantiate the changes. Small, incremental changes that build with a larger strategy. Take what you've learned about the curve of change and natural resistance, then design an approach to dismantle resistance piece by piece. Bringing others along one conversation at a time.

And remember, everyone gets it wrong at some point. The amazing capacity that humans have for expression is matched only by our ability to screw things up. Even when we know better. Especially when we know better.

But if people can adapt and incorporate 14 different words to order coffee, they can do the same to recognize the humanity of another person.

Chapter Three

And Now, the Style Guide

As mentioned earlier, style guides provide an established set of rules around structure and mechanics (comma splices, avoiding repetitive word usage, when to semicolon, etc.). These parameters help to keep your message from falling into chaos.

Depending on the rules, guides can ensure content is accessible, available, and the message easy to consume.

Rules can also have the opposite influence—acting as a gatekeeper to keep things as they are. A mechanism that avoids change based on ideas that the key holders don't like, understand, or are ready to give up on. Guides can silence diverse perspectives; controlling who is represented and how.

Remember, your intention in designing a message is to **bring people in**. It's not about you. This is about considering all the different ways of being.

> "You keep using that word. I do not think it means what you think it means."

—Inigo Montoya, from *The Princess Bride*
(Reiner, 1987, 16:25)

Avoid Using Andronormative (Male as the Default) Language

You thought people had big feelings about the Oxford comma? Brace yourself, this one gets spicy.

Andronormativity is the habit of using "he" or "him" to describe an unknown person. Or using "man" to represent a generic person (manpower, *occupation*man, all men are created equal, mankind, man-made, etc.).

I started using this term to describe the tendency to use masculine words for non-male humans, roles, or titles (fireman, guys, servicemen, etc.). It also illustrates an unconscious worldview that assumes "male" as the default setting when representing humans.

While this might seem negligible at first—like, seriously, aren't there actual problems to solve in the world—take a minute and consider the power of our implicit bias. The words used to describe something will influence how humans interpret and apply meaning to it.

The true crime audiobook I mentioned earlier is a perfect example. The unknown suspect is "he," absent any evidence. This is imprecise. More importantly, it influences any investigation and erases a significant population from the narrative.

And this isn't limited to serial killers or unsolved crime sprees.

Andronormative language shows up a few ways. If you're using words like manpower or man-hours to describe effort, pull the lens back. Consider what you are trying to convey and how it might be experienced as someone who is not you.

Find more precise terms for occupations than just adding "man" at the end (such as, "Wow, that police officer looked surprised when they clocked me doing 94 in a Prius").[3]

Words that inexplicably include gender and some alternatives:

- man-hours, manpower -> resources, estimated time
- unmanned -> crewless, unstaffed
- man-door -> service door
- mankind -> humans, people
- manhunt -> search

Remember to notice the absences. Ask yourself who isn't being represented in the message when you rely on default words. There are a multitude of spaces where humans are erased through language. Yet, we can change that.

Stop Using "Guys" When You Mean "People"

There are also social components to andronormative language. The words that we use shape our understanding, not

---

[3] True story. Fun fact, you cannot take a tax deduction for the cost of incurring a speeding ticket even though it's used as an example in a workshop. Trust me on this.

just of ourselves, but how we interact with each other and interpret ourselves in the world.

For non-male humans, using the word guys is presented as social rounding up (as in numbers, not collecting animals into an organized fashion). You should be OK with being referred to as guys because that's a social elevation into the group. Just as long as you're good with erasing who you really are in the world.

This doesn't work when I address the same gender diverse group by saying "ladies" because it's rounding down. Not just rounding down to the "women" category but rounding down to an even more limited social expectation of "ladies." Now I'm telling you who you are AND layering on restrictive attributions and acceptable behaviors as well.

Don't believe me? Try it sometime. Start off your next budget meeting by greeting everyone in the room with "Hey, girls!" or "Good morning, boss ladies!" The reactions you get will vary. However, they will be different from the non-reaction you get from saying, "guys."

My own experimentation with this resulted mostly in awkward chuckles and confused facial expressions. One team picked up the charge and created an accountability norm to break their old habits. Another time human resources sent me an email asking that I be "less confrontational."

What I'm saying here is that your actual experience could open conversations or close doors. Use what you have available to notice the absences, influence change, and amplify perspectives.

"Wait a minute," you might be shouting, "our entire team is composed of men. So using guys is perfectly fine then, yes?" Yes. Yes and no.

Let's go back to the team who changed their norms and stopped using "guys" for everyone. Yes, if your entire department is composed of men and you know this directly (as opposed to assuming), it's technically OK to use guys.

Developing habits around language isn't only for those who are here now. You are establishing language for those who aren't here yet.

What happens when someone new joins the team? Everyone has to change and disrupt their patterns. Seems like a small thing, but each time they stop or rephrase it's a reminder that the new person is different from them and the group. That new person is then faced with a choice: either defer to the group's established norms and act as if it's not important or continue to be reminded that they are different and they changed the group dynamic simply by showing up.

The group had to change its behavior to be inclusive, rather than being inclusive to begin with.

Boom. There you go. Stop using "guys."

I'd like to take a moment and qualify that boom. If people or groups are unaware that their norms exclude or "other" individuals, they need to do the work to correct the situation. If they push back, gaslight, or pressure the person being "othered" to conform, that's problematic. Again, use what you have available to disrupt, educate, and amplify.

Common "guys" situations and some alternatives

- friend group "guys" -> peeps, friends, folks, folx, y'all, all y'all

- workplace "guys" -> colleagues, team, everyone, coworkers, a version of "friend group" words depending on familiarity, situation, and relationship

- customer service "guys" -> guests, attendees, travelers

- general situation "guys" -> Hi there, Hey, or simply start talking if there is not a clear option available

Use this as an opportunity to create more robust greetings like, "Good morning, all of you amazing humans!" Getting into the habit of finding more precise words disrupts your brain's autopilot. Pause and consider how to describe individuals. Are they colleagues? Students? Conference attendees? Folks?

Using Pronouns—Refer to People as They Really Are

Hallorann: Mrs. Torrance, your husband introduced you as Winifred. Now, are you a Winnie or a Freddy?

Wendy: I'm a Wendy.

Hallorann: Oh, that's nice. That's the prettiest" (from *The Shining*; Kubrick, 1980, 25:22).

Pronoun: a word that represents and stands in for a noun to prevent repeated use of that same noun.

Noun: a person, place, or thing.

There are two types of pronouns in the English language—impersonal and personal.

Impersonal pronouns refer to either inanimate objects ("The lamp—it's broken") or a general collection of unknown others ("One is well-advised to avoid breaking lamps") or ("It was snowing on the day I broke that lamp").

Personal, in this context, indicates the pronoun used represents a person. These are also commonly used in reference to non-human sentient beings, but we're focusing on the human experience here.

So when we discuss pronouns, those used to represent a specific human are defined as personal pronouns.

This distinction is important because not everyone uses "he" or "she" pronouns. It's easy to confuse personal pronouns—used to represent a specific person—as some kind of choice that others get to determine for that person.

I have a name. You don't get to decide my name. Technically, my parents decided that. However, if they'd gotten it wrong, I have final say. Given my general demographic stats, it's a safe bet to assume that my name is Jen. I also get "Tiffany" a lot. Not entirely sure I agree, but it happens. My friend, Tiffany, looks exactly like a "Tiffany" to me. Maybe that's why it feels confusing.

Anyway, pronouns.

Pronouns are a form of representation. Like the true crime audiobook, grouping everyone under "he" erases people who aren't "hes." There was a world full of "shes" being ignored by grammar. Additionally, there continues to be a world full of humans being ignored when pronouns are limited to only "he" or "she."

You don't have to understand it or memorize an infinite list of pronouns. But you do have to uphold other peoples' humanity (as well as your own) by using words that come from them. Notice the absences, as well as who is being represented and how.

Pronouns are not some scientific measurement of being human. They are words that represent or stand in for nouns. In this case, a specific person.

Other people don't get to decide which word that is, except in reference to themselves.

I use she/her pronouns. Again, given my general appearance, most people would assume those are my pronouns. That doesn't mean they get to decide pronouns for me. If someone uses other pronouns in reference to me, I correct them. After that, basic human dignity and respect compels them to use my pronouns. It's not a preference. Any more than using my name is optional if someone feels more comfortable calling me "Tiffany."

When and How to Use "They"

Use "they," a singular nonspecific pronoun, when gender is either unknown, unknowable (for example, talking about someone in a hypothetical situation), or immaterial to the message.

"They" is also used as an individual pronoun. When someone indicates using "they/them/theirs" (or a variance of these) pronouns, it's not a preference. These are their pronouns.

Before we go down a potentially contentious grammar path; yes, "they" is acceptable as a singular gender nonspecific pronoun. It's accepted as scholarly writing style by the American Psychological Association (APA) as of its 7th edition publication manual (Lee, 2019). The Modern Language Association (MLA) also accepts this in its standards (MLA, 2020), as does the Associated Press (AP) (Easton, 2017).

Using "he or she" to represent all humans is imprecise. It also communicates bias. It automatically puts everybody into one of two categories because that's how those who designed the rules understood the world. Again, using "they" isn't implying that there aren't men and women. There are men and women. But there aren't **only** men and women.

Think of it this way:

He = there is one (default way of being)

He/she = there are only two (although "he" has preference)

They = there are more (other ways of being, lived experiences outside of your own)

We put gender in a lot of places that it really doesn't need to be. If it feels like you absolutely must specify "he or she," ask yourself why it's important to know. What happens without assigning gender to hypothetical people or complete strangers? Does it influence how one person would treat or interact with another?

If a delivery driver comes to my shop and leaves a notepad behind, do I need to introduce gender? "They left a notepad" is the message; gender is immaterial.

Using "they" also prevents our brain from developing groundless narratives. Unconscious bias takes over when we encounter gender specific pronouns. We apply a predefined set of traits, behaviors, and value judgments based on our biases, which are not a reality. "They" creates a blank slate that minimizes the conjuring effect. The brain doesn't have a story to hang onto.

Imagine a potential candidate reading through a pre-hire agreement and encountering language like the examples above. It's going to appear (accurately) that the messages are not inclusive. Which calls into question other areas that might not be welcoming.

> "The employee agrees to provide his materials in a timely manner."

> "Employee will track his/her billable time each week."

> "Each employee will submit his or her own timecard by 3 p.m."

The message applies to all employees, regardless of their gender. So why include it here?

Remember, as humans we tend to process information in expected patterns. People who are organized around "he/she" might not interpret this as exclusion, or even notice the usage.

Except you are designing messages that will be available to a broader audience.

If using "they" as a singular pronoun makes you cringe, practice until it doesn't. If the APA can adapt "they, them, theirs" to their style guide, so can you. Once you get into the habit, using "they" is faster and more reflective. It also illustrates how frequently gender is immaterial to the actual message. For example, "If a client is waiting, ask if they'd like something to drink." Or "The librarian will be back soon. They are checking on an order for me."

Using "he/she" eliminates different ways of being. It's a concession stemming from an outdated time when "he" was the accepted representation of humans. And, to your potential employees, partners, and customers, using only "he/she" reads like a dial-up modem sounds. Remember connecting to the internet over dial-up? That grating mechanical sound? The waiting? Right. Time for an upgrade.

Ways to share and respect others' pronouns

- Share your pronouns instead of immediately asking others for theirs. If they want to tell you, they will.

- Avoid creating an expectation that people have to share their pronouns. We're all at different places, and not everyone will feel safe sharing. Especially when they are new to the workplace or environment.

- Start to notice when you assume someone's pronouns based on their name, role, or presentation.

- Protect their data. If you are collecting pronouns, secure these the same way you would other personal information.

Think Through Greetings, Honorifics, and Titles

Honorifics and titles are typically used in an introduction or salutation. Common honorifics are personal (Ms., Mr., Mrs.), or indicate professional titles (Dr., Capt.).

On the surface, this seems straightforward. Include a list of honorifics and have people select theirs. Except, with language and humans, it will never be that concrete. Personal honorifics are more than just titles. They signify different aspects of the person.

- Mx. is gender nonspecific and does not indicate marital status

- Ms. indicates gender (female) but not marital status

- Mr. indicates gender (male) but not marital status

- Mrs. indicates gender (female), implies age (older), and marital status (married)

- Miss indicates gender (female), implies age (younger), and marital status (single)

Much like "he" was historically declared the more correct default pronoun, "Mr." is usually set as the default honorific. If Mrs. is indicated, that person's title becomes "Mrs. + whatever the Mr.'s last name is."

The bigger question here is why any of these matter to your organization. Is there a clear reason or benefit to a user for them to provide this information? This is kind of like the "ladies and gentlemen" habit we covered earlier. Are you veering into a "Dear Sir or Madam" mode of communication? I'm resisting the urge to mention a dial-up modem again, but you know where this is going.

Is asking for Mr., Ms., Miss, or other titles important to the user? Or is it a carryover from 50+ years ago when indicating social status was interpreted differently? Because with most aspects of representation, it is way too easy to get it wrong.

Organizations collect these titles through multiple channels (registration forms, customer surveys, account creation, etc.). The challenge is providing a list that is representative, without causing a user to scroll endlessly or be required to select one before continuing.

Elements to consider when collecting honorifics

- Evaluate the form for bias (options listed for Pastor or Reverend but not other faiths, "Mr." as the default selection, "Mx." not included as an option, etc.).

- Include "Mx." as the first option ("Mx." is a gender nonspecific honorific).

- Use "please select" instead of populating a default honorific.

- Avoid making it a required field.

- Provide a free-text option for users to indicate.

This is a good spot to revisit the two questions: What are you trying to convey and how might it be experienced?

Greetings are another area traditionally influenced by gender, status, and individual experience. For this section, I encourage you to think about greetings on a spectrum of familiarity. Some languages (German, French, Spanish for example) have separate structures for communicating based on the situation and relationship (formal and informal). We need distinctions like that for greetings as well.

Words that are intended to signal respect could unintentionally offend or exclude. Neither of which will support your message. So the less familiar you are with someone, the broader that greeting should be. Ladies and gentlemen, gents, peeps . . . these aren't inherently good or bad. However, they are words and words convey a meaning.

Demonstrating respect is about the recipient, not you. A more universal sign of respect is creating space for them. You won't realize a seemingly innocuous greeting is disrespectful until it's experienced by the other person.

People especially struggle with sir and ma'am. That's a tough one – I get it. So many people from different backgrounds have sir and ma'am deeply ingrained as a sign of respect. Like it's not even an option.

Consider greetings in this light: your intention is to show respect, but if the greeting causes offense, who benefits? If your priority is to reach people where they are, then use a wider lens of options.

If your true intention is grounded in politeness or honoring that person, a more respectful option would be to avoid sir or ma'am unless you already have that level of familiarity. Otherwise, be prepared to occasionally get it wrong.

Capitalization—Race, Ethnicity, and Groups

Time for me to get real for a minute. I considered leaving out this section on capitalization. Not because it's unimportant— this is a critical element of representation. I wasn't thinking about omitting it due to any lack of different perspectives— multiple experts and other style guides have published their positions. I definitely have my own thoughts and approach. The hesitation came from a place of trying to provide objective guidance.

We can't talk about representing humans without acknowledging inherent power imbalances. Humanizing content and messaging starts with prioritizing the lived experience of others.

It's essential to learn, put in the work, and be intentional in usage. Explore and understand the implications of that decision. Resist the temptation to fall back on a series of grammatical rules. These are humans, not comma splices.

Realize that you are probably going to get it wrong at some point. That's part of the learning process.

This section includes sources, their positions, and reasoning provided by each. These sources are not exhaustive.

I intentionally decided to present positions from three organizations: The Associated Press (AP), American Medical Association (AMA), and American Psychological Association (APA).

There is no shortage of opinions on capitalization out there. As with any situation involving complex and uniquely human experiences, our understanding will continue to evolve. If the intent is to reduce bias and negative connotation, my recommendation is to follow APA and AMA guidance. Exception being for quotes and personal expressions that are discussed further down.

The Associated Press

In July 2020, the AP released an updated style on capitalization.

> AP's style is now to capitalize Black in a racial, ethnic or cultural sense, conveying an essential and shared sense of history, identity and community among people who identify as Black, including those in the African diaspora and within Africa. The lowercase black is a color, not a person. AP style will continue to lowercase the term white in racial, ethnic and cultural senses. We also now capitalize Indigenous in reference to original inhabitants of a place. (AP, 2020)

Their statement on the change included this reasoning:

> After a review and period of consultation, we found, at this time, less support for capitalizing white. White people generally do not share the same history and culture, or the experience of being discriminated against

because of skin color. In addition, AP is a global news organization and there is considerable disagreement, ambiguity and confusion about whom the term includes in much of the world.

We agree that white people's skin color plays into systemic inequalities and injustices, and we want our journalism to robustly explore these problems. . . . But capitalizing the term white, as is done by white supremacists, risks subtly conveying legitimacy to such beliefs. (AP, 2020)

I disagree with their phrasing to describe that lighter skin tone "plays into systemic inequalities and injustices." White people benefit from their skin color AND it perpetuates (not plays to) systemic inequalities and injustices. Now might be a good time to revisit the section on navigating awkward silences and discomfort.

APA and AMA have slightly different perspectives than AP since they tend more toward a research or academic style.

In APA and AMA, Black, White, Hispanic, and similar terms are capitalized when used as proper nouns. These words are used as a categorization of people into groups. This is different from describing a generalized population or amalgam of previous experiences.

Keep in mind, since AMA and APA are primarily used within a research, survey, sampling environment, there are other pieces of information to give context. Other aspects of the surveyed population would also be included—such as geographical location (rural area in Alabama, residents of Tokyo, etc.), age range, or similar profile information.

That said, the lowercase "w" is used as a personal expression to create an emphasis or to note a more generalized way of describing a collective. This usage conveys an observable trait, and the underlying degree of access and entitlement associated with that trait.

American Medical Association

The American Medical Association also updated their style guide in July 2020. Its position was described by this release:

> But the terms black and white have been lowercased as racial designators (because they are not derived from proper nouns).
>
> The committee has concluded that we will now capitalize both Black and White, which aligns with the capitalization preference applied to other racial/ethnic categories. We acknowledge that there may be instances in which a particular context may merit exception to this guidance, for example, in cases for which capitalization could be perceived as inflammatory or otherwise inappropriate. (AMA, 2020)

American Psychological Association

The American Psychological Association's direction was initially published in 2019. Its practice is defined below:

> Racial and ethnic groups are designated by proper nouns and are capitalized. Therefore, use "Black" and

"White" instead of "black" and "white" (do not use colors to refer to other human groups; doing so is considered pejorative).

Likewise, capitalize terms such as "Native American," "Hispanic," and so on. Capitalize "Indigenous" and "Aboriginal" whenever they are used. Capitalize "Indigenous People" or "Aboriginal People" when referring to a specific group (e.g., the Indigenous Peoples of Canada), but use lowercase for "people" when describing persons who are Indigenous or Aboriginal (e.g., "the authors were all Indigenous people but belonged to different nations"). (APA, 2019)

It's important to note that in a study or survey context, participants often self-select. They are opting into a specific categorization provided in the survey. Making the use of free-text options in your study design is even more meaningful.

To support that, APA includes this guidance to reduce bias:

"Whenever possible, use the racial and/or ethnic terms that your participants themselves use" (APA, 2019).

Merriam-Webster provides an overview of race and ethnicity, including a brief history of how each developed.

"Today, race refers to a group sharing some outward physical characteristics and some commonalities of culture and history. Ethnicity refers to markers acquired from the group with which one shares cultural, traditional, and familial bonds" (MW, 2021).

Chapter Four

Representing Humans

One of the most common pitfalls in representation is how to do it authentically. Who is being represented and how they are portrayed is a key difference between authentic and formulaic representation.

Remember:
Conjure = internal processing + positioning (images + text)

Our brain is constantly using filters to attribute value and meaning based on our biases. Representation—authentic representation—disrupts these filters. Absences and representation based on stereotypes reinforces existing beliefs. Complicating things further, words combined with images have greater influence on reinforcing our beliefs about ourselves and others.

I'm adding a third question to go along with "What are you trying to convey? How might I experience this as . . . ?"

When you are creating or reviewing content that depicts humans who aren't white males (or present as masculine), evaluate how they are being portrayed in the design: Are they there to serve a purpose, fulfill a role, or are they represented as just living their own damn lives?

Stick with me here.

Avoid Default Settings

The bias toward "male as the default" language also shows up in images and representation. There is a lot behind this tendency—not being aware, lack of diversity in the images available, repeatedly using the same image formula, etc. When I encounter this imbalance, more often than not it's unintentional. At least on a conscious level.

In other situations, content reflects how the person who designed it understands the world. Or how the person approving it is more comfortable viewing the world.

These cases usually follow a pattern:

- White males without observable physical limitations tend to be included by default.

- They tend to be represented in multidimensional ways more frequently.

- Humans who are not white males are generally represented as serving a purpose or fulfilling a role. They are the mom, the buddy, the neighbor, or the assistant.

It's almost as though one needs to reach a standard of social status before they are recognized as uniquely complex humans, with a full story of their own.

The supporting role phenomenon also occurs in communication without images. A common example is attempting to create empathy or humanize an issue by describing women as "people's mothers, daughters, wives, etc." This framing positions women as acquiring value through their relationship to others, rather than inherently having value as humans.

When reviewing content for representation, include an assessment of the roles each person is depicted as portraying. You don't need to run this through a formula or measure against a quota. That approach will eventually result in content where representation feels forced. Instead, look at the "whole" of the content—does it reflect the nuance and complexity of being human? Does it depict humans as themselves, rather than a stereotype grounded in appearance? That's a good starting point for creating layers of representation.

In practice:

- Include a wide variety of ways to be human (different abilities, body types, ages, skin tones, adaptations, appearances, etc.) as well as variety across each individual experience.

- Consider influencing factors (image placement, surrounding and supporting text, etc.).

- Use images and providers with multiple dimensions of diverse representation.

- If your image provider has limited or outdated selections, find another one.

Watch out for:

- Posture or poses that shrink feminine appearing humans, while masculine appearing humans occupy space.

- Placement or proportions that conjure negative perceptions, reinforce biases, etc.

- Images that perpetuate stereotypes.

- Reuse of images (yes, people notice).

Not quite convinced on the white male as default bias? I get it. If you're skeptical, or trying to persuade someone else, do a quick search on board game commercials. Various compilations of ads illustrate the sheer volume of advertisements where white boys win. One exception is an ad for a game called Connect Four. The girl wins and her brother concedes with the comment, "pretty sneaky, sis." (FuzzyMemoriesTV, 2016). Because of course, if a boy is defeated in the game, it can only be due to her sneaky trick.

Appropriation and Erasure

Merriam-Webster defines appropriation as: "the act or practice of appropriating something that one does not own or have a right to. To take or make use of (something) without authority or right" (MW, n.d.).

Appropriation usually involves three elements: 1) misinterpreting the meaning or intention; 2) repurposing that word, ritual, belief, or item without acknowledging the original source; 3) applying or describing unrelated items or situations.

Essentially, people in the dominant culture see something "cool" and take it for their own without a second thought. Often applying their own meaning, while disregarding its actual meaning and the culture who created it.

Appropriation shows up when people call an impromptu work meeting a "powwow." Or describe anything as their "spirit animal." A group of supportive friends or like-minded people is not "finding your tribe." Being an expert in finance does not make someone a "guru." While some words, rituals, or ideas can be experienced by people outside of the community, that is an opportunity to appreciate. It's not something to which one is entitled.

This is difficult for some people to reconcile. Moving through the world when nearly everything is designed by you and for you shapes an impression that it is all available to you.

Pull back the lens.

Appropriation from traditionally marginalized populations is all too common. This taps into centuries of inherent power imbalances, exploitation, lack of social or political influence, enslavement, and systemic injustices. This aspect of appropriation deserves more focus and attention than will fit in this book. However, that doesn't excuse anyone from educating themselves.

Do your research before representing a word, belief, or similar from another culture or segment of the population.

Accurately represent any images or specific depictions. Then, remember to reference and credit that segment or culture. Provide a source for others to learn about it. Include respectful and informed context around any significance or meaning.

Things to avoid:

- taking things that don't belong to you (this includes words)

- applying your interpretation to items, rituals, concepts, or words that belong to others

- using or presenting these without reference to the original culture or source

- any attempt to modify these to fit your needs or align with a belief system

Stigma

This section provides an overview of common stigmas that creep into daily language. It is not exhaustive, and in many cases, specific examples are not provided. This is intentional for a couple of reasons.

First, breaking down the reasons behind stigma can be complicated and very nuanced. Second, these words and expressions can create a multitude of "but, I . . ." defenses. Rather than focus on dismantling every possible argument or attempt to capture a seemingly endless list of words and expressions, I opted for an overview of key areas.

Drug use and addiction

Using "crack," "heroin," or similar drug-related words to describe things like cake or iPhone applications are common examples of this. Even really good cake is not going to result in the depths of devastation and disparate sentencing guidelines as crack cocaine.

More information on the history of crack cocaine and disparate sentencing practices is available in the 2015 report, *Impact of the Fair Sentencing Act of 2010* (USSC, 2015).

Things to avoid:

- stereotypes that assume drug use, abuse, or addition among specific populations

- drug use, abuse, or addiction as an insult

- the word "crack" to describe something other than a specific form of cocaine

Mental health

People are being more open about their mental health. That's a good thing. Casually using words based in stigma makes this difficult. As does pathologizing behavior or actions absent a clinical diagnosis. Being an asshole doesn't make someone a "narcissist." Reducing prices on your Etsy store doesn't make you "crazy." Liking things in a certain order doesn't immediately qualify as "obsessive compulsive disorder" (OCD).

Things to avoid:

- medical terms to label behavior, appearance, or body type
- words that perpetuate stigma or stereotypes
- outdated or dehumanizing terms
- inaccurate, unrelated words to describe situations ("the end of that game was crazy," "this week has been insane")

Infectious diseases

Words shape our understanding and how we interpret new information. This is especially true when that information conveys a potential threat to our health and safety. Remember, as humans we want to find a way to protect ourselves from harm. Part of that instinct is to determine the source or cause of the danger. There is also an element of cognitive dissonance—our brain trying to preserve its belief that the bad thing won't happen to me because of "x."

The way potential threats are described shapes how we unconsciously perceive risk, as well as how we attribute blame to both the source and any impacted populations.

Our brain can oversimplify: if the threat is primarily impacting a segment of the population who isn't me, then I should be safe. If there is enough distance from the source of this threat and me, then I should be safe. Unfortunately, this belief is as ineffective as it is pervasive.

Negative outcomes from this stigmatization are evident in the HIV/AIDS epidemic. Initially referred to as the "gay cancer," later GRID (gay related immune deficiency), the disease was weaponized and used to perpetuate bias against the LGBTQ+ community.

The Centers for Disease Control and Prevention (CDC) began using the term AIDS (Acquired Immune Deficiency Syndrome) in 1982 (HIV, n.d.), by which time the general perception of this as a "gay man's disease" had already taken hold. Instead of being addressed as a public health crisis, this disease would become fodder for elected officials and late-night comedy segments.

So words matter, especially when they involve describing potential risk to one's health and safety.

To address this phenomenon, in 2015 the World Health Organization (WHO) advocated new guidelines for naming infectious diseases (WHO, 2015). These practices include more precise word choice and avoiding reference to specific regions, cultures, and a variety of elements that can invoke human bias.

Things to avoid:

- downplaying the social and economic influencing factors on health disparities

- promoting research or data without reviewing the original source

- using terms or expressions that demonize or stigmatize an illness

Beyond Cringeworthy Words and Expressions

I was on a conference call that started off like any other meeting. Pleasantries exchanged. Questions about everyone's plans for the weekend. The usual. Things were moving along as expected. Seemed like we might even wrap up early.

And then . . .

Throughout this book, I've mentioned the frequency with which you will experience awkward silences while doing this work. "Awkward" is an occupational hazard, as is negotiating difficult and emotionally charged discussions. Except some conversations—and the phrases that spark them—can include surfacing traumatic historical events or periods.

This meeting took an unexpected twist as one product manager was describing a new gaming device. Another product manager suggested that their colleague's enthusiasm was because they "drank the Kool-Aid." Three minutes later I was looking at a screen of faces; humans who were learning about the horrific tragedy known as Jonestown.

I have decided to exclude details on the events related to Jonestown in this section. Primarily to avoid triggering or unintentionally causing upset. Researchers and documentarians have explored Jonestown to a depth that I can't capture here in a few paragraphs. Trying to describe it in less than a full account would be a disservice, and disrespectful to all those who were impacted.

If you choose to keep using the expression "drink (or don't drink) the Kool-Aid," you have a responsibility to understand the origin and its implications. For those who are interested in learning more about this absolutely terrifying part of U.S. history, resources are included in the book's reference section.

How they can show up: (actual instances observed in the workplace since 2021)

- describing stressful situations or pressure to deliver (tightening the noose, cracking the whip, slave driver)

- describing long or sustained periods of effort, extensive overtime, or a long travel day (death march, back to the salt mines, gulag)

- describing anything as "ghetto," "gangster," or being "sold down the river"

- describing security filters as whitelisting (to allow) and blacklisting (to exclude or block)

- describing distributed systems or relationships across devices as "master/slave"

Avoid:

- using expressions without understanding their origin story and underlying meaning

- assuming that everyone is OK with these expressions and knows what you "really mean"

- prioritizing your familiarity and habit of using these expressions over the incredibly horrific violence they represent

- erasing uncomfortable truths and horrific events to make history more palatable

Chapter Five

Workplace Learning and Training Content

When was the last time you completed a required training course at work and the experience wasn't horrible?

I'm not talking horrible in the sense of painful or scary (whatever that means to you, reader). I'm talking about experiences that are stereotypically bad. Bureaucratic dystopia kind of bad. Experiences that are worse than scary—they are *shudders* boring and likely involve getting lectured. Paperwork. Sacrificing your time, possibly money, for the sake of meeting a requirement.

Activities like going to the Department of Motor Vehicles because you forgot to renew your driver's license on time. Showing up for jury duty. Waiting in line behind people making small talk with the cashier when all you want in life is to pay for your Coke Zero and get back on the road. OK, that last one might just be me.

But what if you had geared up for this soul-crushingly boring and potentially miserable experience, only to find that it didn't suck? What if it was actually informative and . . . wait for it . . . optimized for humans?

What comes to mind when you think about mandatory training in the workplace? Or when you get an email reminder from Human Resources about completing that 45-minute course? You know the one. Those off-the-shelf courses that cover "Respect in the Workplace," "Anti-Harassment," "Safety Awareness." All the old favorites.

These courses are necessary for legal/regulatory compliance, but they can also be good. Effective. They can **bring people in**. The challenge is that bad is accepted as normal, until you know what good looks and feels like.

Content in these mandatory courses influences how people perceive themselves within an organization. Yes, in many cases the material has to meet specific legal requirements. The course design itself? That decision represents what is top of mind for leadership.

The content style and presentation establish a baseline of expectations. They also communicate what the priorities are. Selecting content for mandatory employee courses is going to convey what the organizational culture is really all about.

Is It Legal-First or Human-First?

I want you to distinguish between workplace course designs that use a "legal-first" focus versus "human-first" focus.

A legal-first approach to content is exactly what it sounds like. These courses promote a central focus on legal definitions, thresholds, and degrees of behavior.

Courses that use a legal-first approach tend to lead with definitions and categorizations. Harassment is defined. Protected class is defined. Characteristics of those included in protected classes are defined. This framework can create an "us" and "them" mentality in groups that are already dysfunctional or unhealthy.

Content using a legal-first approach frames toxic workplace behavior as, "Does it meet the legal definition of harassment?" or "Is the person being targeted part of a protected class?" Both questions are necessary, but they don't address or educate employees on behaviors that meander right below legal thresholds. So, the message conveyed to employees is about avoiding risk and evaluating interactions against legal criteria.

Legal-first courses typically close with a lengthy, but nonexhaustive list of nasty behaviors that cannot be perpetrated against the "thems" and why those behaviors are prohibited (because of legal protections—the company is obligated to prohibit them if they want to avoid being sued).

Feels a little gross, doesn't it?

When you encounter employee-facing content with any of these features, treat it like a 99-cent shrimp cocktail in Vegas and back away.

Let's unpack that for a minute. The legal-first approach, not the shrimp cocktail. I didn't even get that from *Bar Rescue*, it's just good life advice. Like never splitting a pair of tens.

Using a legal-first message to build a respectful workplace culture looks like this:

Harassment = protected class + shitty behavior.

What about shitty behavior that isn't directed at (or involving) a protected class?

When workplaces use a legal-first approach to human interactions, diverse representation can be resisted and weaponized as: "I can't say anything (do anything, treat you like everyone else, be myself) around you without getting in trouble."

Complicating things further, for many individuals, it might not be immediately evident that they are included in a protected class. Which puts the burden on an employee to disclose and share potentially intimate details. Additionally, legal protections have little to no benefit in organizations, communities, or environments which are unsafe for that individual.

If your content follows a legal-first approach, this indicates fulfilling a basic legal obligation. It's a transaction. A condoned level of acceptable workplace behaviors because you made everyone review the course and take a quiz.

This approach also lends itself nicely to groupthink, gaslighting, and pressure to conform. Legal-first frameworks address the policy and regulatory aspect of a workplace (compliance) without establishing an intentional culture (good humaning).

Human-first content design is different. It's grounded in the uniquely human need to be psychologically safe and "seen." People want to be valued for who they are in the world. They want their workplace to provide them with a shared understanding of the rights, responsibilities, and systems in place to protect everyone.

Human dignity and respect are first. Protections, rights, responsibilities, and the process to uphold are baked in throughout.

Cultivating an environment that brings people in is good for humans, necessary for innovation, and a more effective business model. Content with a human-first approach accomplishes both objectives.

"But, Jen," you might be shouting into your coffee mug, "we have to mention harassment and protected classes! It's a legal requirement! We'll get fired!"

Maybe you do need to mention that. I don't know, I'm not a lawyer. You probably do. But is your goal with this course to meet the most basic requirements to which your organization is legally obligated? More importantly, is that your intended message to employees?

Because if that is the goal and intention, then your company's value statement begins and ends with "because we're legally obligated to do this." Which you are, but "legally obligated" is not a value statement. Unless your desired company culture is "whatever keeps us out of litigation."

You do need to make legal protections evident. You don't have to leave it as the only message conveyed or re-traumatize employees in the process.

Lead with an unapologetic, "We operate in a respectful environment because we value good humaning." This doesn't mean that everything will be great. It won't. It's going to be super awkward and frustrating at times.

That's where the undertone of **"We respect each other first"** will out-perform, out-innovate, and out-problem solve "because a video told us we had to" every time.

"Training" Content vs. "Learning" Content

Training and learning are often used interchangeably, especially in the workplace. For the purposes of this section, I want to make a distinction between training content and learning content. Yes, training is learning. Both can be terrible or great. Both are necessary in the workplace. However, there are specific elements in learning content that make it worth separating here.

Training courses tend to cover how to perform a task, operate a system, or complete a defined process. Things like learning to operate a forklift, or how to request time off in your employer's tracking tool. How to reduce the risk of someone losing a digit when working with equipment. There is less of an emotional component to training.

Workplace learning and professional development courses tend to cover human interactions. There are more variables and fewer absolutes. The goal is to influence employee behavior by providing information that will (hopefully) motivate them toward good humaning. Whether the topic is embezzlement (spoiler: don't) or fostering a more collaborative team, learning involves less "contained process" and more "humans are squishy and complicated."

Since learning courses explore these squishy, complicated human-centered topics, the material tends to tap into different nerves than training courses. The subject areas are more personal and relatable. We can visualize ourselves and others in the scenarios. Except not always in a positive light.

Put another way: a "Safety in the Workplace" training is different from a course on "Respect in the Workplace." People are less likely to have an involuntary emotional response when taking a course on general safety. Confronting their biases and examining nuanced decisions about behavior? Those are more likely to surface some complicated internal dialogue.

Workplace courses have an exceptionally short shelf life. Reviewing content from even 5 years ago feels like moving back in time by decades. It's like watching episodes of the 1980s television drama *Dynasty* and hoping it resonates with all your employees.

These courses typically follow a standard model. There is a "happening" (some example of inappropriate action, decision, or behavior), followed by:

- 1 person speaking out against the bad behavior and/or supporting the person subjected to the happening

- 1–2 people going along with, or minimizing, the happening

- 1–2 people who are uncomfortable, but avoid, ignore, pretend not to notice because of reason x (which is explained through the narrative)

- 1 manager or person from human resources who is dismissive at first, but then comes around and supports taking action against the happening

- employee has to take a quiz or speculate about the happening

The content also tends to rely on overt examples in these happenings. Like a caricature or regulatory violation brought to life. Demonstrating the dangers of bribery with a cartoon villain, who sneaks in with giant bags of money. Currency symbols printed on the sides and everything.

The feeling associated with these formulaic models is often: "I have to watch this because it's required."

Except, "We're doing this because we have to" isn't going to inspire people to change how they interact. At least not in a way that aligns with the culture you're trying to create.

Bad learning content persists because companies continue to purchase it. Those in a position to influence decisions might not realize that it could be good. Maybe they know that great content is out there, but introducing change seems too overwhelming (expensive, time-consuming, etc.).

Except bad content has bad outcomes. And many of the negative outcomes associated with bad learning content can go completely unmeasured. Complaints can be dismissed as, "Well, no one likes training" or taken under advisement, but with no action. Something the company should address "next time," when there is a new provider, or more budget, or fill-in-the-blank event that never seems to materialize.

So, where to start with all of this?

What Are You Trying to Convey?
How Might I Experience This As . . . ?

When you're evaluating learning content, consider what messages are conveyed. This might be a good time to refresh on all the various factors that influence our biases. As well as how humans can conjure meaning that isn't explicitly part of the message itself.

This includes the words you use to describe these courses, both directly to employees, and behind the scenes during your selection or design process. Words influence and shape our perceptions. So is it legal-first "Mandatory Anti-Harassment" or human-first focused "Respect in the Workplace?" Do you people still refer to the course as "Sexual Harassment?" Shifting your language, even in seemingly minor instances, will change how people approach this material.

I'm not suggesting you create an elaborate euphemism. Those are annoying. But be precise in word choice or that culture of legal-first mediocrity can seep into your organization.

Show them the transformation in a culture of respect and what it feels like to be part of that.

Similar to the earlier section on reviewing content in layers, there are multiple elements involved with learning courses.

Level 1

- Does the message invite employees in, or give them a list of things "not to do"?

- Does the content lift them up? Or warn them how not to "get in trouble"?

- Does it follow the "happening" model described earlier in this chapter? Or does it involve a more nuanced approach?

Level 2

- Who is being represented and how? Legal-first is grounded in avoiding litigation. Check for stereotypes, bias, lack of diverse representation (outside of the "protected class" section).

- What is the baseline? Does the message assume (and subconsciously expect) the worst of employees?

- What is being depicted? Does it follow a series of reenactments of toxic behavior? Are you requiring employees to engage with content that is damaging or harmful?

I encourage you to sit with the uncomfortableness of that last question for a minute. Then ask yourself, what else is this content conjuring for people?

Harassment Content Doesn't Need to Be Creepy

Imagine sitting through a required course on workplace bullying as someone who grew up experiencing domestic violence. Being compelled to watch 60 minutes of anti-harassment scenarios as someone who narrowly escaped sexual assault at their last company, or as someone who is currently being targeted by another employee in your organization.

The concept of triggering previous trauma is rarely a focus in mandatory workplace courses. Yet, most courses on anti-harassment use scenarios where actors reenact highly distressing exchanges. Then, employees are quizzed on the unsettling event they witnessed.

Above all else, employees are humans. Humans who have their personal histories coming along to work every day. Some of your employees experience post-traumatic stress disorder (PTSD), could be survivors of assault, might have been targets of bullying in previous workplaces—all of which influence how they navigate the world.

We tend to think of people in the workplace as being completely separate from their individual lived experience. As though our colleagues show up for work without having the decades of everything that's happened to them coming along for the ride.

When people are exposed to bullying or toxic behavior (as the target or observer), they process it through their previous life experiences. Our brains pick out the most familiar association of situations where we have dealt with this feeling before. Watching similar situations can become a flashpoint.

Some people will freeze or appear to not notice as a coping mechanism. They may act oblivious with the hope that it will go away without their involvement.

Consider the number of people who experience violence, bullying, or similar traumatic events. There's an exceptionally high probability that a segment of your employee population is coping with this to some degree.

Potentially harmful content requires informed consent. Trigger warnings and content warnings serve a purpose: to protect the reader or audience from being exposed to content that could cause them harm or distress. Or at least provide this information in advance, so each individual can make an informed decision.

I'm not rolling this out as an expectation that you'll become an expert in trauma response. But it's important to understand what happens when your learning material contains depictions of toxic behavior. Or other elements that carry potential harm.

If you are unfamiliar with, or would like to learn more about, physiological responses and how the body processes trauma, additional resources are listed in the reference section.

Trauma is exceptionally complex. And far outside of what I can describe here.

At a very layperson level, triggers are things the brain or body have specifically associated with a trauma. The stimulus (trigger) initiates an involuntary response in the body. As a protection mechanism our brains will "fast-track" or prioritize our responses. The person's body is ready to escape, hide, cry, dissociate, or whatever kept them safe in earlier situations.

Triggers can include sounds, motions, spaces, scents—even ones commonly perceived to be pleasant, or any combination of these and myriad other elements. They can occur in a momentary flash and can cause the person to feel as though they are back in the situation or experiencing the trauma again in real time. Triggers reactivate the trauma response, resulting in an unexpected rush of feelings, such as anxiety, fear, panic, and helplessness.

Now imagine asking a survivor of trauma to watch a 60-minute video of a real-world reenactment of toxic behavior. Or disclose their concerns about the material and cope with whatever outcomes. This is not an approach that supports humans.

Since trauma is so intensely personal, it is critical that you avoid labeling or speculating about what others are experiencing. It's important to stay aware of these potential reactions to content types. Use this information to reduce the risk through more effective approaches.

Again, more details and resources from experts are included in the reference section. If you are feeling overwhelmed, help is available by texting or calling 988, the hotline that gives you 24/7 access to trained crisis counselors if you're experiencing suicidal thoughts, substance use, a mental health crisis, or any other kind of emotional distress.

Chapter Six

Find It and Fix It

Now that you're equipped with all this information, let's move to the next stage: finding and fixing areas of your content that don't support your message or those who interact with it.

Hopefully by this section you've had time to experience a few episodes of *Bar Rescue*. It's not necessarily a required activity in order to get through this book, but the show manages to illustrate the process of humans interacting with change really well. The relationship that people on the show have with rationalizing their resistance is also eerily similar.

If the bar owner says, "This place is fine" while we're all looking at the same nonfunctional glass washer and two inches of standing water, that's a disconnect we need to explore.

If I'm outlining the racist undertones and negative stereotypes in an employee training course, and the client says, "The content is fine, we can't replace it because of x reason," that's also a disconnect we need to explore.

The effort starts with going through those hard-to-reach places where bias, stereotypes, or other barriers like to hide.

Buried in the content that nobody reviews because either it's too mundane, overwhelming, intimidating, or *shudders* just not sexy.

Organizations tend to focus on externally facing content, often prioritizing something with more visibility. It's easier to articulate the potential value of a new campaign and catchy tagline to put on the side of a bus or a banner outside the building. These are the big, interesting initiatives that get everyone's attention. People can rally behind them, and executives rush to allocate resources. Except interesting and big don't necessarily translate to impactful or lasting.

As tempting as it is to start with something more obvious (or sexy), I invite you to focus here first.

Small Changes and Big Perceptions

Why am I asking you to start with changing content that nobody seems to care about? Great question—stick with me for a minute.

When my sister and I lived in the same city, we'd work out together. We'd go for a run on Saturday afternoons, meet for indoor cycling, or do an early morning CrossFit class. One day we decided to try out a barre class. The sessions incorporate elements of yoga, Pilates, and ballet. It seemed straightforward and, while neither of us are particularly coordinated, we figured it was worth a try.

During the intro, we were directed to pick out hand weights. They started at one pound each. One. Pound. Two, if you can hold both in the same hand. We openly mocked the tiny weights and charged directly to the heaviest set. If I'm being honest, we may have even flailed the smaller weights around making dinosaur noises. Why bother with something not worth the time invested in class?

Six minutes. We made it six minutes with those heavier weights before slinking over to exchange them for three pounders. The shame. We brought this on ourselves.

Our downfall was thinking that we'd understood the assignment. Our hubris was based only on our previous workout experiences, which involved using heavy weights for shorter periods of effort.

But barre is about balance, precision, and sustained work. All while not falling over, which is a focus that requires some serious effort—at least for me. These were smaller movements using lighter weights for what seemed to be around 17 hours. Turns out it was 6 very humbling minutes. Lesson learned.

Is it satisfying to finish a heavy set of deadlifts and shout "FUUHHHHGG!" when you're done? Of course. But don't underestimate the impact of those small-but-mighty lifts that appear so easy until you're the one doing them.

The small, incremental changes I'm outlining in this book are your metaphorical 3-pound weights. Your personal version of metaphorical 3-pound weights can be anything. Maybe it's a toaster. Or a wombat. Entirely up to you. The point is to find something that represents a feeling of precision, balance, and sustained effort.

These toaster wombats are building you up for more complex and substantial work later on.

Using this strategy will encourage your brain to:

- Overcome fear of an action by incremental exposure and practice.

- Train your "muscles," and everything else that goes into an action, how to do the action.

- Build on that with the next challenge.

These incremental changes tend to be more in your immediate control. There is likely less friction and a sense of overwhelm. Another bonus: starting here provides a more contained learning space.

You're going to make mistakes and miss things. We all do—it's part of the journey. Prioritize form and consistency over a briefly satisfying "FUHHG!" Build on these smaller changes and connect them across your longer-term strategy. Remember, "FUHHG!" can quickly result in an injury if your body isn't ready. There will be points of heavy effort and working beyond what you think is possible. That comes later. For now, focus on sustainable effort and small, incremental changes.

And this is why I'm inviting you to start with content that nobody seems to care about.

This approach also supports:

- getting smaller pieces out of the way, while developing your technique

- shifting your perception, making the more nuanced elements easier to spot

- expanding how you think about this aspect of design, so you can explain to others why change is necessary

- understanding how much of the content "nobody looks at" is actually required for people who work with your organization (employee guides, mandatory training, onboarding processes, legal agreements)

Working through more prominently featured content follows a similar path. You start to notice these "little things" everywhere. Then suddenly, more subtle or nuanced elements emerge. Your brain is filtering information through a different lens. This is where the small-but-impactful changes begin to connect.

It's like working on a giant puzzle. At first, everything looks the same. Then you start filling in the edges and connecting a few obvious pieces. As your brain adapts to the orientation, you'll start to spot patterns. Then the connections across bigger and more abstract pieces become clear.

Your toaster wombat changes are also opening the door for others to consider things differently. The process of changing these small things sparks conversations, curiosity, and opportunities for a variety of new perspectives. Creating this momentum makes it an easier sell to policy influencers, executives, or decision-makers who are resistant to these changes or change in general.

Curious to find out what could possibly be lingering in those boring, unsexy pieces of content that no one really reads? Great, follow me.

Start by Looking Behind the Refrigerator

Imagine you had somebody completely deep clean your kitchen. They do everything: steam the walls, bleach the grout, polish the fixtures. Everything. It's glorious.

Except they didn't look behind the refrigerator. So all that stuff that's been collecting—the stuff that nobody bothered to clear out year after year—is still there funking up your glorious kitchen. It's there and getting worse by the day. Even if all you experience is a room full of lemon-fresh grout, someone will notice that funk behind the fridge.

That funk behind the fridge is all the bias, stereotypes, and exclusionary wording in your content. It likes to hang out in materials that go unnoticed or are actively avoided. In true *Bar Rescue* form, we're about to find out what's up with that grease trap. Brace yourself, it's about to get real.

Here are a few top places to start (or, if you're really feeling bold, do a reverse sort-by-date on your content section in SharePoint):

- pre-hire and new hire forms
- policy documents
- legal agreements
- employee guides and training material
- textbooks and manuscripts
- learning and professional development courses

- registration forms (check your third-party applications as well)

- employee or customer satisfaction surveys

- messaging for call centers, guest reservation desk, and support services

Basically, start with things that somebody will have to review maybe once every couple of years.

I know, I know—this seems like a list of content that nobody cares about, other than maybe legal, human resources, and compliance teams. Are you sure that's the case?

As I mentioned earlier, most of these items are required at some point in the life cycle. They may even be part of the earliest encounters people have with your company. And the more mandatory an experience with content is, the more likely it will be allowed to be soul-crushingly bad. Because what choice does the person have except to comply?

You have to check every interaction point because it's these micro-experiential blips that truly tell the story. And the "funk" might be all that they will find.

It helps to first understand what people hate about interacting with your company, and then find ways to disrupt it. Improving the experience includes details like an employee onboarding resource that doesn't induce migraines and fatigue. Or revisiting job postings that emphasize the importance of going out for beer with the team. Yes, really. These are still out there, lingering behind more fridges than you'd expect.

These materials are often one of the first messages to new employees, potential business partners, or the talented candidates you are trying to attract. Are you serving them up documents that are monolithic chunks of legal jargon sautéed in Times New Roman because "nobody really reads these anyway"?

Sadly, this is where the refrigerator metaphor starts to fizzle. Cleaning out the funk of whatever happened before is much easier in the kitchen. Figuring out what to look for in content is more nuanced. So, now that you know *where* to find it, how do you know *what* to fix?

Excellent question. Buckle up.

Fix it

This process is about examining content in layers. Design placement, word choice, images can each be problematic on multiple layers. There can also be multiple elements that need to be separated out. Items that are great individually, but problematic when combined. The further you get into this aspect of design, the more things start to surface. It's a process.

I sectioned the concepts by first and second level. This grouping does not indicate hierarchy, prioritization, or value. Breaking these out makes it easier to start identifying what needs updating. It also separates different design areas. Trying to unwind all these elements at the beginning stages can be overwhelming.

Depending on the work you do, some areas may not apply directly. I encourage you to get familiar with them anyway. The same applies if you are not directly involved in the day-to-day efforts of design. This can be helpful information for future use or to know what to consider during development. You can find visual examples of these in the extra content at www.Paging-DrJen.com/BehindTheBrand.

The first level includes:

- bias, erasure, stereotypes, exclusionary language

- outdated or inaccurate usage of terms

- placement and combination (conjuring)

- phrases and expressions with negative origins

- appropriation, objectification, tokenization

Beyond bias, exclusionary terms, and conjured meanings, barriers to your message can also include:

- fonts that are difficult to read or stressful for humans to process

- dense blocks of text and competing focal points

- overly complicated language (beyond jargon and internal acronyms)

- overwhelming combinations of color, varying font size or style, moving images, sound

Neglect eventually results in materials that are full of bias, erasure, stereotypes, exclusionary language. These can be very subtle and nuanced—outdated terms, formulaic images. They can also show up as a big 'ole "he" as the only pronoun right up in your face.

> "The employee agrees to provide *his* materials in a timely manner."

> "Employee will track *his* billable time each week."

These are actual sentences, taken from an employee agreement dated 2022.

Continuing to use "he" as a default pronoun isn't any great mystery. This is the result of formalized writing standards presenting "he" as more correct and clearer. Generations of writers were conditioned to use "he" as the pronoun unless additional context required using "she."

Traditional writing guides, such as *Elements of Style* promoted "he" as being a generic representation of humans for decades. Assuring people that "he" should be used as the standard pronoun as recently as 2018—looking at you, *Elements of Style: Classic Edition* (Strunk & De A'Morelli, 2018, pp. 81–82).

Bias can also show up in places like a list of honorifics. Think of registration pages using a pre-populated list with "Mr.," "Mrs.," and "Miss" as the only choices. Or worse, limited options with "Mr." set as the default selection. If you present users with a defined list that excludes them, you are going to lose people.

I've encountered this experiential glitch when reviewing:

- online employee applications

- hotel and restaurant reservation pages

- ticket sales and retail platforms

- vendor registration sites for companies seeking "diverse suppliers"—yes, really

- companies that actively promote the importance of diversity in their supplier base with registration forms that default to "Mr."

How does using "he" or "Mr." as the default setting align with your company's values? More importantly, what are you intending to achieve in collecting this detail? However insignificant it may seem, each step in your process is asking potential customers to give up two things: time and personal information. When the data only benefits you, that's annoying. If it only benefits you AND is exclusionary? That is where the company will start to lose people.

I realize it seems like a small thing to pick on. So much going on in the machine, why spend energy on a few words amid hundreds of others, buried across countless other documents?

Because the words that live in these forms and online spaces represent you. They signal everything about your company, about you as the creator, and what it's like to work or do business with the organization.

Instead of This, Try This

These points in the experience are easy to miss during design. Start looking here—in micro experiential blips that may be the only place someone interacts with your content. Consider those two elements: What does this convey to the person registering, and did anyone explore how it might be experienced?

Example 1:

Registration: Step 3 of 4
Please indicate your gender
☐ Female
☐ Male
☐ Other

Here are a few layers involved with the example above:

- Listing "male," "female," and "other" is offensive. Humans are not "other."

- Limiting people to one of these choices dilutes your data. You will know which option was selected, but not who the person actually is in the world. This is where a free-text option and "prefer not to answer" are more welcoming, while also providing better insights if customers chose to share.

- Skewed response population. You are only gathering data on those who didn't abandon when encountering these options.

Let's go back and evaluate against, "What are you trying to convey?" Or, in this case, "What are you hoping to extract?"

- What is the relevant bit of information?

- Why is it necessary at this point of the journey?

- What insights are you expecting to gain?

- Who do you envision would check the box indicating "other"?

It's dehumanizing, yet so preventable.

So, instead of this . . .   **Try this . . .**

Registration: Step 3 of 4
Please indicate your gender
☐ Female
☐ Male
☐ Other

Evaluate why you need to collect gender
If there is a credible need: - indicate as an optional field - provide an opt-out choice - use a free-text field

Another common example of exclusion shows up in options listed for titles. Enrollment or registration pages that list "Pastor" and "Reverend," but not "Rabbi" or representation of other faiths. How might this be experienced? Is it possible the designer included options that are most familiar to them?

Less is more in these situations. Again, ask yourself what is the intended use of this data? It's adding another step to the registration process. From a privacy perspective, this also requires potential guests to share another level of personal information.

Honorific fields should be left open or set with a "please select" label. While the option list can't be exhaustive, it should be inclusive. Consider including an open text box and let them tell you.

It takes time and effort to fix these seemingly minor issues. You'll get resistance and pushback. Most organizations don't intentionally neglect their message or secretly want it to be off-putting to potential customers, clients, and employees. However, that's what is happening here.

What if Your Content Is Terrible?

Yeah, this section can be a tough one. Going back through your earlier content can feel like diving headlong into a series of yearbook photos with less-than-ideal fashion choices. Imagine reading through your journal entries from two decades ago. Were things really that raw? Yes. They were for you at that specific moment in time. Based on what you knew and had available to you.

Acknowledge the cringeworthy, and then do better.

Disclaimer: This section addresses the general range of cringeworthy content and messaging. Racism, sexism, misogyny, using your position to demean others—these have severe and long-lasting negative impacts on humans. Comments and images in this category normalize damaging behaviors. They also carry a splash and ripple influence across society.

When your message causes damage or harm, it needs to be rectified. What that means depends on a variety of factors.

For now, apply this section to content that you now understand as biased, exclusionary, or cringeworthy.

So, what to do when your content is terrible?

The important thing to understand is that at some point, you're going to get it wrong. This applies whether you designed the content, purchased it, or were involved as a decision-maker to roll it out. It isn't a matter of if, it's when and to what degree. The approach I suggest is to pause and take a breath.

When you first realize that the content is problematic, take a few minutes and reflect. These realizations can be followed by some pretty intense emotions. We're accustomed to an occasional typo or using the wrong word (*discreet* and *discrete* get me every time), but this realization is different.

It's the sudden recognition that your content caused another person to feel "less than." And coming to terms with the unanswerable question—how many times has this happened before?

This can feel like a panic response as your brain looks for a way out. Hard thoughts to wrestle with, but it's part of the process. Have the existential crisis—experience all the things—then get back to the work of exploring new viewpoints and integration.

As humans, our first reaction is usually to defend ourselves or explain what we wanted to happen. Our brains immediately try to protect the ego and become dutiful press agents. We go into damage control with some version of "That's not what I meant," or "I'm not that type of person," or any possible objection that might prevent you from feeling discomfort (and embarrassment) that comes with hurting someone.

So pause, take a breath, and really evaluate the feedback you are getting. Think about the lived experience of the individual who has been harmed, damaged, or diminished by your message. This requires some heavy work on your part, along with a lot of being humble, human, and realizing that you don't know what other lived experiences are like.

How you meant it is irrelevant. The message is interpreted based on that individual's prior experiences and how the world interacts with them. Without stopping and listening to what the problem is and how to address it, you will continue to get it wrong. And once you're aware of problematic content, you own being part of the solution.

Then, apologize. An unqualified and uncomplicated apology. Don't make it about yourself, your intention, what you meant to convey, or how you wish it would've been communicated. Whether it was intentional is irrelevant. Focusing on intention shifts attention away from the damage, and toward your experience of the message itself. Sit with that for a minute. Expressing intention makes the apology about *your* experience, instead of the resulting harm to others.

Apologize. "This was a mistake. Here's what we're doing to resolve it." Then commit to the work involved in doing better. It's a journey and a process.

If you're not sure how things went wrong, or you are genuinely not sure why people are reacting in a certain way, reach out. Find a credible professional with expertise in that area who can advise you. Leverage the many resources that provide guidance, advice, and education.

One caution: It's tempting at this stage to become what I like to call an "unconsented to champion." This is when one has an almost overwhelming desire to pick up a metaphorical sword and charge up the hill to right all the wrongs for marginalized humans everywhere. And it usually ends badly.

Take another pause and consider what else might be happening here. Is this an overcorrection to give more immediate satisfaction? Is taking this direct charge action distracting you from processing uncomfortable feelings? Did the population you're attempting to serve invite or ask for support?

Other than this approach being completely unsustainable, it can cause a lot of unintended harm to the population you are hoping to help. My suggestion is (for now) to keep focused on your own process, work the 3-pound weights, and build relationships in those communities that you want to support.

Because, once you "see" it, you own being part of the solution. That requires a lot of heavy work, a lot of being humble, and using what you have available to influence change.

Chapter Seven

What You're Up Against

I was on a video call with a colleague (in the Before Times when this was less common). During a side conversation they expressed an opinion that was very surprising to me. Definitely not a position that I would have expected this person to believe, let alone say out loud to someone else.

It took a second to process the experience of what I'd just heard. My counterpart appeared to be processing as well. Two people blankly staring at monitors, both pretending to have connection issues to buy them time to think of something.

Previous conversations I'd had with this colleague flashed in my mind. How they must have internally reacted to the experience of trying to reconcile what I said with their impression of who I was in the world.

I realized that when I've said something that conflicts with another person's belief system, they'd likely gone through the same processing that I was doing now. The process was happening for both of us. They were evaluating this new information against who they imagined me to be.

The other person was experiencing me and possibly thinking to themselves, "How on earth can she believe that? It's so obvious."

While I was looking back at them thinking, "How on earth could you believe that? It's so obvious."

Exchanges like these can spark an internal dialogue to try and reconcile. It goes like this: "We get along and have a personal connection, how can you believe something that directly conflicts with my beliefs? If I have strong feelings about people who believe what you do, what happens now?"

I even imagined them talking about it with friends over happy hour. "Can you believe it? I know she's from Seattle and all, but seriously."

Yes, my brain went there. We are always the hero in our own narratives.

It's so tempting to lead with a direct response that both supports your position and undermines theirs. To shut the other person down. This isn't to say that one should never shut down another person's expression. Bullying, harassment, threats—shutting these down is an appropriate response if you can safely intervene. However, what about in the example with a colleague stating a position that conflicts with mine?

How you respond in each of these moments depends on a lot of things. Which is why I recommend staying present and assessing the question: To what end? What are you trying to achieve in the moment, and what is your intended long-term outcome? What are possible consequences (to you or others) if the situation escalates?

Directly charging at people with the message, "Everything in your belief system, everything that you grew up knowing, everything that kept you safe—it's all wrong. Now, you have to change all of it" is less effective than one would think. Is this approach satisfying? Sure, it can be. But is it effective after the fact? Rarely.

It's also unlikely to gain any lasting ground. Humans don't respond well to an existential undoing. It's an automatic response to dig in and reinforce "I'm right." The ego wants to protect itself. Consider the longer-term objectives and how those align with the situation in front of you.

In the video call example, my first inclination was to launch a full charge. Direct rebuttal. Clearly, my position on this matter is correct and I just need to convince you.

Over time, and after many more awkward situations, I realized the effectiveness of a pause. Pulling the lens back before responding. Taking a minute to consider what was in direct conflict—my beliefs or my perspective? Establishing your approach in curiosity helps discern whether to "charge" or focus energy on drawing connections. Don't get me wrong— charging back is necessary at times, but this is about an effective approach over one that only serves as immediate gratification.

Pause and reflect before peeling back their objections. What is coming up for you? For them? For the team or others involved in the situation? Give everyone space to express their resistance. But not so much that it becomes toxic or damaging to individuals, the team, or their environment.

Think of it like measuring the pH level in the soil because your plants are shriveling up. If the conflicting ideas are within a healthy midrange and the team has established boundaries, you're more likely to get positive outcomes from active exchanges. Too far in the extreme, or if the team environment is toxic to begin with, it might be time for a direct charge.

The Curve of Change

Under the best circumstances people don't like change. Or they like change right up until it impacts them or makes them reevaluate how they view the world.

Frustration is your brain's best weapon in preventing change. We begin to resist at the first itch of this essential part of growth. We become so accustomed to deflecting this discomfort, eventually it becomes habit.

But for the purposes of this book, that discomfort is what I want you to notice. The more unsettled you feel at the prospective change, the closer you are getting to the actual "why" behind it. Pushing through this discomfort means exploring the deeper reasons. Peel back and evaluate the stories we tell ourselves about why things can't start changing.

As you start applying some of these ideas at work, there will likely be change resistance. Even from those who are fully on board and advocating right beside you. You're operating inside of a system with other people. The best defense (other than a good offense) is understanding how humans interact with change.

A few things to think about before we start:

- When the body becomes anxious, our first instinct is to establish normalcy.

- The urge to maintain "normal" can keep us stuck by shutting down actions that trigger negative feelings.

- Learning or incorporating new information can be mentally, emotionally, and physically draining.

Huge oversimplification alert

So, this is the curve of change. It's a generalized visual to represent how we process new information such as change. Specifically, when that change, or new information, is perceived to have a direct impact on us at an individual level. Our brains navigate this nonlinear journey through shock, denial, angst, uncertainty, and "what-if" scenarios. Hopefully, we break through and make it to the upward cycle toward integrating this new information.

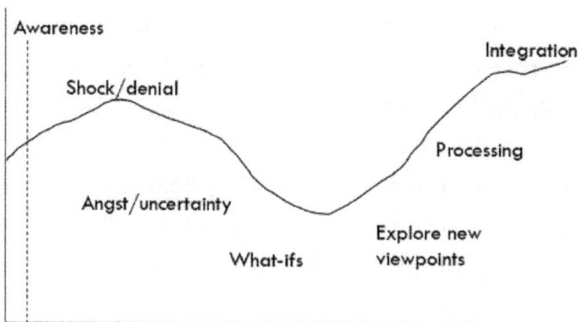

The process starts with what I like to call a "happening." *Phenomenon* might be a better word, but people can get hung up on the science-y feel. Fun fact—both words are movie titles.

This *happening* can be anything from an unexpected layoff notification to your favorite spot for lunch going out of business. It can also show up in rumors or suspicion of an impending change. Happenings based on rumors or speculation go through a more complicated process because those put our imagination in the driver's seat. Anything goes as we look for clues, signs, and omens about what could be around the corner.

Once the happening has actually . . . erm . . . happened, our brains work to interpret and make meaning of it.

We tend to follow the same processing model for both significant changes and minor annoyances. Your brain goes through this process even when the happening involves a change to the layout of your favorite social media platform. Everything is in a different place, and now you must invest time adjusting to a new color scheme, icons instead of words, or new password requirements.

Your brain becomes frustrated and goes through the curve of change. Three weeks later you likely won't even remember what the previous landing page looked like. The change has been successfully integrated. Ta-da!

We all go through this to varying degrees. The time and energy invested varies depending on magnitude, perception of control, and our individual capacity or relationship to change.

The brain goes through the curve of change when:

- Your employer introduces a new system that requires additional training.

- New leadership or a reorganization is announced at your company.

- Road construction results in a detour that adds 3 minutes to your daily commute.

- You accept an exciting new opportunity that requires moving across the state.

Remember, there doesn't actually have to be a change for our brains to spiral. Sometimes the hint of a change is enough to set our minds into motion. These cases are more complicated because imagination takes over to fill any gaps and ratchet up the what-if/angst stages. It's like those scenes in horror movies that don't show all that is happening. Our imaginations are infinitely more powerful than what can be captured on film (and the scare factor is personalized to what is front of mind for each of us).

Let's take a look at each of the stages. Keep in mind, this is a nonlinear process with a variety of influencing factors along the way.

Awareness: This is the initial exposure to the happening. It starts the evaluation and assessment process. You know that something (real or adequately speculated) is coming. Now it's all about what could be involved and how it impacts you.

Have you ever noticed that company layoff announcements typically have an extra paragraph or two after the impact statement? Those closing comments following the key message serve a purpose. They're a buffer to give people something to consume while the brain is processing awareness.

From there, we spill headlong into . . .

Shock/denial: These two are so closely related that I'm keeping them together. Your brain has acknowledged the happening and is looking for a way out. It churns on any hope that this change can be avoided or prevented from being. The realization that life and our understanding of it before said happening might be gone forever.

As the brain cycles through each possible exit strategy, we start to deal with . . .

Angst/uncertainty: At this stage, people often revert back to shock and denial. Depending on the magnitude and impact of the change, it can take a while to break through. We need more information and time to evaluate. This is also where that desire to shut down change can bubble up. The brain attempts a return to normalcy by whatever means possible. Usually by deflecting new information and avoidance.

Which brings us to . . .

What-ifs: This is where our imaginations really start to shine. As humans, we are extremely creative and can come up with all kinds of different scenarios. Our brain spins up a multitude of ways that this change could impact every aspect of life as we know it. Then we try to problem solve all of those at the same time. This process picks up at our most vulnerable times. Typically around 3 a.m. or when we are least equipped for clear action.

Unfortunately, this is where people tend to get stuck. Even more so than the previous two stages. They continue to cycle between uncertainty and "what-if." Each time they get close to the next stage ("explore new viewpoints") something causes a shutdown.

This is where business leaders and change agents can make a difference. Pay close attention as people get to this stage. Notice how they are talking about the situation. What words are they using to describe it?

Our words, and the words used by others in our immediate environment, inform how we interact with uncertainty. I'm not saying to frame the change as all sunshine and roses. However, when the team is surrounded by consistently negative words, it keeps them stuck. What happens next is critical to breaking out of the cycle. Which is why I'm spending so much time on this stage of the curve.

When teams (or you) are spiraling in "what-ifs," it can be difficult to think about anything else. Having a visual representation of the curve can help people break through. It gives something to point at that says, "You are here" and a sense of what's possible on the other side of the unknown. Then you can envision a way forward that doesn't need to be overwhelming. The first glimmer of hope.

Which leads people to an upward cycle. Starting with . . .

Explore new viewpoints: This stage is exactly what it sounds like. People have taken a pause and are starting to organize the information. Sorting through their "pre-happening" perspectives and getting curious about the positive what-ifs. This stage is a good time to present new ideas and have open discussion about the possibilities.

Processing: Trying out different ways of doing things. Experimenting and exploring the new situation. Enlisting peers and other champions to amplify the benefits of change. Finding a path for people who are stuck at "what-if" or earlier stages.

I want to emphasize that this last point is not about creating a pressure campaign to force people into embracing change. That approach is unhealthy and can encourage toxic behaviors. It's also rarely effective for getting to lasting change. Making room for diverse perspectives—especially those that don't mirror yours—is a necessary component for leading teams through uncertainty.

Integration: Finally, we get to the integration stage. This is when you forget what the old social media landing page looked like. Integration is where you internalize the change. More importantly, integration gets you ready for the next one.

Why is it important to be mindful of this process? Primarily to help you navigate through the various stages, while leading others along their journey. Incorporating change can feel overwhelming and it's easy to get stuck. Understanding what the curve of change looks like can give people hope—there is a way through.

Our Content Is Fine

"Our content is fine." Have you ever encountered this statement? Have you ever said or expressed it? This is a safe place to admit, it's OK. Most of us have been susceptible to, "Everything about how we do things is fine because I haven't had to think about it another way." It's one of the primary reasons that diverse perspectives are key to more innovative problem-solving. Provided you, or the decision makers, are open to views from people who aren't them.

Most companies will fall into the category of wanting to do better, but not sure how or where to start. Others genuinely resist change.

Phrases like "our content is fine" act as a mechanism to shut things down. If this is a consistent refrain within your organization, introducing change can be incredibly difficult. I'm not trying to scare you off. Only suggesting that you evaluate the situation realistically. Companies are a collection of individuals and not everyone is on board for change in general, let alone doing the work that comes along with designing for inclusion.

Any of these seem familiar?

- "We don't have time to fix it."

- "We'll do it starting next quarter (year, after the reorganization, etc.)"

- "It's just that department (group, person), they're always complaining about something."

- "We did an employee survey on that before, and it wasn't reported as a problem."

- "The Leadership team is 'old-school.' They'll never go for that."

- "That's what HR (or DEI team) is here to do."

Think about these like marbles being dropped into a glass vase. One or two? Not so bad, this can be overcome.

Lack of time or resources to improve an entire catalog of employee training? That's valid to an extent depending on the situation. But are these sentiments built into every production cycle? That starts to feel like resistance has become a habit. These statements are a way of postponing change without explicitly shutting it down.

Before you know it, the vase has shattered after being inundated by a constant stream of "now right now" marbles with nowhere else to land. Consistently lacking the time, resources, and dedicated focus to change *everything*—that's a conversation. To change *anything*? That's indicative of a larger problem.

Think about that one for a minute. A common tactic to avoid the discomfort of change is listing reasons why we can't take any action. Building a comprehensive catalog of all the things preventing us from doing something. If there isn't time or resources to act until "x" happens, that delay prevents people from examining why the potential change makes them uncomfortable.

These reasons become our fallback position. The problem with this, other than nothing ever changing, is that these reasons typically don't hold up to scrutiny. It gets uncomfortable in a big hurry.

Examining what is motivating you away from necessary change generates more internal tension and frustration. Sometimes there is almost a physical sensation to it. But that frustration can also signal the beginning of a breakthrough. That's where we get to the good stuff—finding and naming the barriers that keep each of us stuck in our own cycles.

This breakthrough phase makes it possible to do the internal work and unpack those feelings. Then, your real list of next actions becomes much clearer.

What if there isn't an obvious need for your content design, or language, to change? What about when everyone in the marketplace is doing the same thing? Designing toward the same industry standard. Why make a ruckus—an expensive ruckus—about such a small thing?

Because at some point, the industry standard will shift to become more inclusive. This shift will either happen with you, or to you.

Disrupting Business as Usual

Disruptive technologies, economic swings, and global pandemics can flip the ways of doing business faster than a coffee table after accusing Grandma of cheating at Monopoly on a rainy Saturday.

Let's take a look at one of my favorite examples: Netflix.

Back in the late 1990s, Blockbuster and Hollywood Video (hereafter referred to as "BB/HV") dominated the video rental market. Both companies started as a disruption—creating competition for smaller, local rental businesses and providing an alternative to visiting a movie theater.

Stores in these two video chains had more selection than seemed imaginable. Imagine a casino with row after row of plastic VHS boxes instead of slot machines and table games. There were posters, snacks, rental promotions. Even the carpet was a disorienting blur of color and the broken hearts of independent film producers. BB/HV were designed to feel like the full cinematic experience, except you were able to retreat and enjoy movies in the privacy of your own home.

Then Netflix (a small startup at the time) nearly drove them both out of business.

The BB/HV rental model was predicated on people going to a physical store and spending as much time as possible there. Stores weren't designed for efficiency. The longer a customer was in the store, the more they were likely to spend. Especially when there were kiddos in tow.

Except customers weren't being asked whether they enjoyed the experience. People went into video stores because that was the only alternative to movie theaters or cable providers. BB/HV had an advantage over smaller competitors through volume, selection, and add-ons that prevented other errands for customers (snacks, sodas, etc.).

To be fair, some customers did seem to like the in-store experience. They tended to land squarely in the "movie fan" category. People wandering through the horror section with friends, trying to find the slashiest of slasher films. Grownups pitching *For the Love of Benji* like Quentin Tarantino to their kiddos, while holding a bucket of 'Xtreme Butter Blast as leverage in the weekend movie negotiation.

BB/HV didn't consider that people would rather skip the store, or that going into and navigating stores was a barrier all by itself. They didn't consider things that customers hated about this experience, or aspects of the in-store experience that prevented potential customers from engaging. Because BB/HV didn't have to. If people wanted cinematic entertainment, they had to leave the house. How else would it work?

Netflix showed up and completely rewrote the script (no pun intended) on customer experience. The company provided a viable alternative that solved problems BB/HV considered features.

Its model introduced a rental platform that eliminated in-person interactions. The customer simply created an account, curated their list of movie selections, and three days later—voilà! Their movies arrived in the mail. No more hoping their desired selection was in stock. Or on the shelf where it was supposed to be. No more wandering around a store being overwhelmed.

I understand how weird this all sounds to some of you, but at the time it was revolutionary.

Netflix also tapped into other industry standards that customers hated: late fees and the return process. Netflix had a flat membership rate, with no time limits on rentals. Which meant no more late fees. You mailed the DVD back in a pre-paid envelope, and the next movie automatically shipped. No more rushing back to the store. Customers could even share movie lists and recommendations with friends. Community without the hassle of conversation. Perfect!

Great story. What does this have to do with content design?

Companies who view (or lean on) industry standards as a constant, rather than as less-than ideal customer situations ripe for change, are missing opportunities for disruption. Netflix didn't disrupt things by trying to out flash the others. It captured what people hated about the existing models and designed an alternative.

Business leaders miss opportunities to be change agents every single time they design systems without exploring what consumers might hate about it. Worse, business leaders understand that people hate it and rely on a lack of other options available in the market.

Netflix leveraged the smaller and more meaningful details in less obvious places. Places like what people complain about when they think of your business or industry. The best part? These smaller details in the customer experience had more staying power than investing in, say, 150 copies of *Ishtar*.

BB/HV started as disruptive, offering viable alternatives to things people disliked about movie theaters. Then they looked for experience features and new revenue channels that benefited them, not their consumers. They banked on the same customers spending more, (because where else were they going to go?), while ignoring everyone who was unable to engage with them (because why bother?).

These former disruptors relied on a continued lack of options instead of innovating models that could reach a broader, untapped audience.

It's also possible that BB/HV never thought to explore if these potential customers were out there. Studying the profiles of typical moviegoers will give insights on their preferences and behavior patterns. But how do you learn about populations who aren't represented to begin with? People who, for a variety of reasons, must overcome barriers before engaging with your product?

Part of flipping the script on industry standards is exploring what people hate about doing business with you. This includes investigating which aspects of the experience might limit their interactions with your content and product. Easier said than done—I get it. Companies (and people in general) tend to diminish data that doesn't support existing beliefs. They say, "Our design is great because it reflects how the industry expects it to be."

Right up until that next shift.

Chapter Eight

So, Now What?

Throughout these chapters I've mentioned all the things that "you're" going to change. This last one feels like a good place to explain what I mean by that.

The book was intentionally organized as a "choose your own adventure." That approach goes for this closing section as well. You can take elements from here and apply them in your daily work. You could introduce reviews and quality controls to prevent design flaws. Or develop an end-to-end review of customer interactions—fixing those experiential blips that cause both real and metaphorical eye rolls every single day.

You might also decide to flip the script on an entire industry.

Ultimately, this guide is intended to help you spot things that detract from a message, are exclusionary, or create barriers to your content/product. And at the end of the day, you can change things. Your organization isn't something that just fell from the sky. It isn't a function of nature. It's a collection of humans and can be changed by humans.

Keep in mind, people have complicated relationships with change. In part because change requires energy, but also when it taps into uncertainty or feels overwhelming.

Unfortunately, you're also going to encounter those who resist change because they benefit from things staying the same. People who, for whatever reason, would rather keep the existing structure in place.

So, in support of the adventure you chose, here are a few closing thoughts.

Taking on the Dead Things

I decided to take a break from all things digital one weekend and hung out on the deck. I noticed some of the agave plants could use a little love, so I found the shears, put on my headphones, and went to work.

I'm fortunate enough to be dealing with plants in an established garden. Everything was cleanly designed and cultivated intentionally. Blooms were spaced well—optimized for light and water—and organized into an array of colors. The previous owners clearly loved their garden until they simply couldn't keep up anymore. Then time and overgrowth took over, leaving it difficult to see what was initially planted and trying to come in. Side note, this is an actual garden in my backyard, not an analogy. True story.

About an hour in, I realized the similarity between cultivating healthy plants and leading teams of humans. It's not enough to keep the plants alive—I mean, technically, yes, it is—but that's the floor, not a goal. The goal is to have them thrive. That outcome requires understanding the complexities of plants, as well as the nuance of each specific plant.

I bought two small-ish English lavender plants and put them into the same ground, with the same soil, light, and watering routine. One did well and the other died over a period of 5 weeks.

Everything was the same, yet nothing worked to revive the second plant. Even shouting, "Be more like your brother!" had no noticeable effect on either plant. Clearly everything wasn't the same. They were two different plants, from two different containers, with two different origin stories.

As I moved further into the garden's more overgrown sections, the differences in plant outcomes became more evident. Vines and a series of invasive species had taken over entirely. Stronger plants developed in odd directions while trying to compete for sun and water. Some had to be pruned back, others were completely gone.

The vines and dead stuff were keeping new growth underneath from getting necessary resources. **Because that's what dead stuff does.** It creates more dead stuff. Vines pull down other growth causing it to stagnate or die from lack of sunlight. The dead stuff blocks anything new from coming up.

I couldn't help but think about unhealthy workplaces and how resistance or fear of change keeps us stuck in them.

Vines are surprisingly ambitious. They can grow in from different angles and up from underneath other plants.

These invasive species blend in with the landscape and look like your other plants at first glance. Their expansion is only noticeable when you get really close. Maybe you accidentally grab it and end up with a palm full of stickers. Then good luck figuring out which one got you.

The closer you get to their root systems, and the longer you spend in that close-up perspective, the more evident it becomes which plants are lifting things up and which are vines (creating more dead stuff).

The dead stuff doesn't mean that things can't come back. It just needs to be cleared up and evaluated. Not all of it immediately—an entire ecosystem has developed underneath that dead stuff. If you trim dead leaves off a plant all at once, that can kill it. Wait too long and the new stuff will also die off. Not all plants are going to make it, as evidenced by the ill-fated lavender plant I mentioned earlier. Still have no idea what happened with that one.

So, as you're developing a short- and longer-term strategy for implementation, consider picking up a couple of plants as a reminder of everything that's possible.

It's a Human Issue First

One question I've been getting a lot is how organizations invest in changes without being viewed as "political."

My position is that inclusion, diversity, representation, equity, and belonging are human rights issues.

Now feels like a really good time to remind you that I'm not trying to change anyone's belief systems. This is about evaluating a framework—content and communication—that wasn't designed to support or represent *everyone*. Then changing that framework to bring others in.

Over the last few years I've encountered not wanting to be political more frequently. As the momentum from 2020 slows and doing the hard work necessary for change becomes more difficult, organizations seem to fall back on avoiding "politics."

It's often used when describing a confrontational, difficult, and appearing-to-be-unsolvable situation. Not wanting to be thought of as "woke" or taking a "political" position is becoming an easy way out for some organizations.

This (and similar) sentiments come into play when decisions have higher stakes. That's where you come in. You're going to start noticing.

When companies—and the individuals within them—demonstrate principles as human rights, everyone benefits. The same is true for taking positions outside the workplace that uphold individual dignity, respect, and representation.

As you begin to apply some of the ideas in this book, you're going to start noticing not only the content that needs to change, but also the resistance that comes with challenging rules.

Consider who creates these rules, how they are enforced, and which perspectives are amplified by keeping them in place. You might begin to question what's "always been done."

The industry standard. How content is "supposed" to look. Everything you've ever been told about how to write "properly" or what "professional" means in your work.

Because you're about to change them. And show people (including yourself) how things can be better.

Humans have the right to be represented as they are in the world. Without serving a purpose, being objectified, or having their culture appropriated. Humans have a right to encounter others who are like them in textbooks, stories, and organizational experiences.

Humans have a right to exist and be portrayed outside of stereotypes, social narratives, and biased expectations. They have a right to their own stories and lived experience.

The tendency to consider human rights as "being political" is because these topics are often presented only within the context of political discussion. This is especially true with the most basic human rights for marginalized populations.

We've conflated promoting human dignity and respect with "politics." I feel that Neil Gaiman captured this best in his 2013 statement about the expression "politically correct."

> I was reading a book (about interjections, oddly enough) yesterday which included the phrase "In these days of political correctness . . ." talking about no longer making jokes that denigrated people for their culture or for the color of their skin. And I thought, "That's not actually anything to do with 'political correctness.' That's just treating other people with respect."

Which made me oddly happy. I started imagining a world in which we replaced the phrase "politically correct" wherever we could with "treating other people with respect," and it made me smile.

You should try it. It's peculiarly enlightening. (NG, 2013)

Human rights are not political. Inclusion, diversity, and representation are not political. Doing the work to unpack your own bias is not political. Noticing the absences and amplifying other voices are also not political. Challenging structures and designs that negatively impact humans—also not political. Although I get where that last one starts to feel a little like activism, and not everyone is ready for it. Nonetheless, not political.

Before You Go

First, this work is really difficult, and it can feel like things are moving backward at times. It's easy to become overwhelmed. People can fall into the trap of trying to do everything all at once.

Start with evaluating your content, or whatever can be directly influenced. Allow that action to spark conversations with colleagues and others in the industry. Use what you have available and intervene where you can. Practice disruption with a "The image used here is not OK" queued up. You aren't going to change that person's mind, but other people are also watching. And someone will think to themselves, "I need to write that down because I'm saying it next time."

Second, never underestimate your ability to influence. Even if you aren't successful in implementing new approaches, advocating for them creates opportunity. Raising these issues has a splash and ripple across the organization.

You've already instigated change by finishing this book. Your perspectives are different, even if you didn't agree with everything along the way. Especially if you didn't agree with everything. Word choice, images, messaging—all of these will be interpreted through a slightly different lens. That's change. Small, incremental toaster wombat level change.

Challenge formulaic representation, appropriation, and stigma when you encounter them. Use that to which you have access to amplify voices other than your own. Actively seek to build relationships with people who aren't "you." Bring others in to advocate for new standards and practices.

You picked up this book for a reason. Now, let's get to work.

About the Author

Dr. Jen O'Ryan has been humanizing content, processes, and organizations since 2003.

As a consultant and strategist specializing in inclusion, diversity, and representation, Jen works with organizations of all sizes to remove barriers. She combines a PhD in Human Behavior with over 25 years of experience leading organizational change. Her background in the tech industry includes designing new experiences for customers, launching global initiatives, and making order out of chaos.

After an extensive career of instigating change at Fortune 100 companies and a few small-but-mighty startups, Jen created Double Tall Consulting. This new company fills a gap faced by many organizations—how to develop their inclusion, diversity, and representation initiatives from "good intentions" to effective, measurable, meaningful results. Working as a corporate partner, she successfully develops content, brands, and user experiences that are welcoming across a broad audience.

Jen frequently speaks at conferences and events and has recorded podcasts related to building inclusive organizations, navigating resistance, and why humans suck at change. She is the author of *Inclusive AF: A Field Guide for Accidental Diversity Experts*. Designed for anyone thinking about inclusion and diversity, *IAF* outlines a roadmap to influence and lead others through culture change.

Outside of work, Jen is a travel enthusiast and avid runner. She also has a strange affinity for bad 80s music, getting lost in new cities, and scary movies.

You can follow Jen on social media:

www.LinkedIn.com/in/JenORyan
www.Instagram.com/PagingDrJen
www.Facebook.com/PagingDrJen

Working with Jen

Change starts with a conversation.

Dr. Jen O'Ryan is an engaging speaker and facilitator with a gift for making sustainable change more achievable. Blending humor, storytelling, and evidence-based approaches, she brings audiences along on the inclusion journey, meeting them where they are and showing them a way forward.

Whether it's introducing new perspectives and related initiatives, managing through discomfort, or redesigning your organization to be more human-first, Dr. Jen's unique strategy can move your teams from good intentions to meaningful results.

Ready to get started? Learn more about Jen's work or schedule a consultation at www.PagingDrJen.com.

References

Introduction

Elements of Style (EOS). (2023). Wikipedia entry. Retrieved from https://en.wikipedia.org/wiki/The_Elements_of_Style

Strunk, W., Jr., & De A'Morelli, R. (2018). *The elements of style: With editor's notes, new chapters, and study guide.* Spectrum Ink.

Chapter One

Independent Living Institute (ILI). (1999). Retrieved from https://www.independentliving.org/docs3/brown99a.html

Universal Design (UD). (2023). Wikipedia entry. Retrieved from https://en.wikipedia.org/wiki/Universal_design

Chapter Two

British Broadcasting Corporation (BBC). (2022, February 24). Retrieved from https://www.bbc.com/worklife/article/20180723-the-commas-that-cost-companies-millions

Encyclopedia.com. (n.d.). Dandy. In *Encyclopedia.com dictionary*. Retrieved from https://www.encyclopedia.com/ fashion/encyclopedias-almanacs-transcripts-and-maps/ dandy

Merriam-Webster. (n.d.). Dandy. In *Merriam-Webster.com dictionary*. Retrieved from https://www.merriam-webster. com/dictionary/dandy

Merriam-Webster. (2016, August 29). *The left hand of (supposed) darkness*. Retrieved from https://www.merriam-webster.com/wordplay/sinister-left-dexter-right-history

Spacey, J. (2017, June 10). *14 types of design flaw*. Retrieved from https://simplicable.com/design/design-flaw

Chapter Three

American Medical Association Style Insider. (2020, July 1). *Updates to reporting black and white as racial categories*. Retrieved from https://amastyleinsider.com/2020/07/01/ updates-to-reporting-black-and-white-as-racial-categories/

American Psychological Association. (2019, September 10). *Racial and ethnic identity*. Retrieved from https://apastyle. apa.org/style-grammar-guidelines/bias-free-language/ racial-ethnic-minorities

Associated Press News. (2020, July 20). *Explaining AP style on Black and white*. Retrieved from https://apnews.com/ article/archive-race-and-ethnicity-9105661462

Easton, L. (2017, March 24). *Making a case for a singular 'they'*. Retrieved from https://blog.ap.org/ products-and-services/making-a-case-for-a-singular-they

Kubrick, S. (Director). (1980). *The shining* [Film]. Warner Brothers.

Lee, C. (2019, October 31). *Welcome, singular "they".* Retrieved from https://apastyle.apa.org/blog/singular-they

Merriam-Webster. (2021, June 21). *The difference between 'race' and 'ethnicity'.* Retrieved from https://www.merriam-webster.com/grammar/difference-between-race-and-ethnicity

Modern Language Association. (2020, March 4). Retrieved from https://style.mla.org/using-singular-they/

Reiner, R. (Director). (1987). *The princess bride* [Film]. Act III Communications.

Chapter Four

FuzzyMemoriesTV. (2016, December 18). *Connect Four – "Pretty Sneaky, Sis . . ."* [Video]. YouTube. https://www.youtube.com/watch?v=KN3nohBw_CE

HIV.gov. (n.d.). *A timeline of HIV and AIDS.* Retrieved from https://www.hiv.gov/hiv-basics/overview/history/hiv-and-aids-timeline/

Merriam-Webster. (n.d.). Appropriation. In *Merriam-Webster.com dictionary.* Retrieved from https://www.merriam-webster.com/dictionary/appropriation

United States Sentencing Commission. (2015). Retrieved from https://www.ussc.gov/research/congressional-reports/2015-report-congress-impact-fair-sentencing-act-2010

World Health Organization. (2015, May 8). *WHO issues best practices for naming new human infectious diseases* [News Release]. Retrieved from https://www.who.int/news/item/08-05-2015-who-issues-best-practices-for-naming-new-human-infectious-diseases

Chapter Six

Strunk, W., Jr., & De A'Morelli, R. (2018). *The elements of style: With editor's notes, new chapters, and Study Guide.* Spectrum Ink.

Chapter Eight

Gaiman, N. (2013). *I was reading a book about interjections.* Retrieved from https://neil-gaiman.tumblr.com/post/43087620460/i-was-reading-a-book-about-interjections-oddly

Printed in the USA
CPSIA information can be obtained
at www.ICGtesting.com
JSHW011130130524
63026JS00007B/24

9 798218 386139